World

Rockers Swagger

by

Glenn Johnson

Chapter One

Christmas Day in Agrinio, Greece, was a quiet affair for the lads in Swagger the mods and Swagger the rockers. The Christmas Eve party had gone really well. The Freddo coffee helped to perk everyone up for a long night, and the music played until nearly 5 am. The air was mild. It wasn't freezing. It wasn't snowing. It wasn't icy. But there was a slight breeze in the air, and Santa Claus would be on his way to deliver presents to everyone before it got light.

The ouzo that had been consumed in large quantities would help to knock the partygoers out, as they drifted off home, and Ted, Sid and Fred, along with their girlfriends, the stunning dancers and beauty queens, Jilly, Jackie and Rosie stumbled into the Aris Hotel, that was located opposite the Lord Byron Memorial Hall. Rob, Rick and Cyril also shuffled to the Aris Hotel, along with the equally beautiful dancers and beauty queens, Lily, Erica and Becky.

The Lambretta scooters outside zoomed off in all directions, taking home the mod revellers, and the Norton and Triumph motorbikes sped off in various directions, ferrying dozens of rockers towards their living quarters.

Ted, Sid and Fred's parents had earlier retired to bed. They couldn't cope with staying up after 10 pm. And they disappeared into the hotel shortly after 10.30 pm. They had seen what they wanted to see, namely their sons playing live on stage, and they had thoroughly enjoyed it.

Roger Daltrey and Steve Marriott stayed at the bar, chatting, and drinking Freddo coffees, planning the next stage of the tour.

Following a brief Christmas holiday for two days, on Christmas Day and Boxing Day, the party left Agrinio in Greece for Kenya. Ted, Sid and Fred, along with their three women, and Rob, Rick and Cyril, with their three ladies, travelled back on plane. They couldn't travel by van, as they were due to play a gig on New Years Eve in Nairobi, in Kenya, and they needed time to practice, set up their props and arrange their set. So an aircraft journey would give them valuable breathing space and time. They loaded their equpiment on board the aircraft and travelled in style. No bumpy, tiresome, seven day road trip this time. The plane would only take 10 hours to fly from Greece to Kenya. Sid, Ted and Fred's folks continued to travel with them too, and remained a calming influence on their offspring. Everyone was looking forward to Kenya.

The East African Airways was the flag carrying airline of Kenya and was jointly run by Kenyan, Tanzanian and Ugandan authorities The headquarters was in Sadler House in Nairobi in Kenya, which was the destination for the Swagger and Swagger bands and their entourage, including Roger Daltrey and The Who and Steve Marriott and The Small Faces, and Swagger the mod band's folks.

This East African airline was the same airline that originally transported them from the UK to Tanzania in Africa, and had done a great job. There were no complaints from anybody, and this journey would hopefully run just as smoothly.

Everything was loaded. The passengers settled down. The plane was Kenya bound. Ted, Sid and Fred were tired, but excited. The Christmas festivities were catching up with them. They had hardly slept. But the beds had been working overtime, and the walls had never been hit so hard by the headboards, as the lovemaking shenanigans with their women, was at a peak. This journey would give them some respite, which was much needed.

Nairobi was looking fine in the late December sunshine, with only 5 days to go before it was 1966. Christmas was over. But there were still Christmas decorations and lights hanging from buildings, and the Nairobi airport was a cluster of lights, decorations and festive goodies.

Nairobi is the capital and largest city of Kenya. The name comes from the Maasai phrase Enkare Nairobi, which translates to "Cool Water" a reference to the Nairobi river which flows through the city. The city is popularly referred to as "The Green City In The Sun." Nairobi was founded in 1899 by the colonial authorities in British East Africa, as a rail depot on the Ugandan railway.

The town quickly grew to replace Mombasa as the capital of Kenya in 1907.

After independence in 1963, Nairobi became the capital of the Republic of Kenya.

During Kenya's colonial period, the city became a centre for the colonies coffee, tea and sisal industry. The city lies in the south central part of Kenya, at an elevation of 1,795 metres or 5,889 feet. It has the Nairobi National Park, with a large game reserve, which was established in 1946 and is 4 miles south of Nairobi. The park has a large and diverse population, with species that include lion, leopard, African buffalo, black rhinoceros, giraffe, hippopotamus, spotted hyena, hartebeest, blue wildebeest, plains zebra, cheetah, Thomson's gazelle, Grant's gazelle, impala, waterbuck, common warthog, olive baboon, black-backed jackal, common ostrich and Nile crocodile. It is fenced on three sides, whereas the open southern boundary allows migrating wildlife to move between the park and the adjacent Kitengela plains. Herbivores gather in the park during the dry season, which are anatomically and physiologically adapted to eating plant material, such as foliage or marine algae, for the main component of its diet, and have mouthparts adapted to rasping or grinding, with wide flat teeth that are adapted to grinding grass, tree bark and other tough plant material.

Mervyn Cowie, born in Nairobi, campaigned for the establishment of a national park system after seeing the amount of game animals on the Athi plains had dwindled. He had recalled this as a place of paradise that was quickly disappearing, and the Nairobi National Park was the first national park established in Kenya in 1946. Cowie was named as the director of the Nairobi National Park and held the position until 1966.

The site of Nairobi was originally part of an uninhabited swamp. With the arrival of the Uganda railway, the site was identified by Sir George Whitehouse for a store depot, shunting ground and camping ground for the Indian labourers that were working on the railway. It had high elevation, temperate climate, adequate water supply and was situated before the steep ascent of the Limuru escarpment and Whitehouse, the chief engineer of the railway was criticised by officials within the government, who felt the site was too flat, poorly drained and relatively infertile. But Nairobi grew from strength to strength and by 1921 had 24,000 residents and 12,000 native Africans.

After World War 2, continuous expansion of the city angered both the Maasai and Kikuyu tribes, which led to the Mau Mau uprising in the 1950's, and a series of Lancaster House conferences initiated a transition to Kenyan independence in 1963.

The tour of The Who, The Small Faces and Swagger the mods, continued. With guest appearances being made by The Kinks and The Rolling Stones, and Swagger the rockers were invited on to the tour of Africa, starting in Nairobi, Kenya. Roger Daltrey and Steve Marriott were so impressed with Swagger the rockers, that they could not ignore their talents, and had to include them in the tour, alongside Swagger the mods. The lads were thrilled and excited and everyone looked forward to the first gig at the Sharon Hall on the edge of Nairobi, with a massive crowd waiting.

The beauty queen dancers, Jilly Jacobs, Jackie Jones, Rosie Wright, Lily Lewis, Becky Bright and Erica Shaw, dressed in skimpy black bikinis, did their thing. Flinging their bodies into all sorts of sensual shapes, strutting their sexy stuff. It was an eyeopener. And it built the crowd up into a frenzy, and the dancers shuffles, gyrations, grinding and cavorting was a feast to the eyes. The concert had begun.

"Welcome to our show!" bellowed Roger Daltrey, as compere. "And hello Nairobi! I hope you're all doing fine! We shall start tonight with The Small Faces, and their song "Sha-la-la-la-lee." This song reached number 3 in the chart, where it spent 11 weeks and was released on 10th February 1966. The guys showcased it for a first time playing in the concert, and it made a fantastic impression.

"Picked her up on a Friday night
Sha-la-la-la-lee, yeah
I knew everything gonna be alright
Sha-la-la-la-lee, yeah
Sha-la-la-la-lee
I asked her, "where do you wanna go?"
Sha-la-la-la-lee, yeah
Well, we went some place I don't know
Sha-la-la-la-lee, yeah
Sha-la-la-la-lee
I held her close and I asked her "if she was, gonna be my baby?"
It felt so good when she answered me, "Oh yeah, oh yeah"
"Oh yeah, oh yeah, oh yeah"
She looked good and she moved so fine
Sha-la-la-la-lee, yeah
And all the guys knew she was mine
Sha-la-la-la-lee, yeah
Sha-la-la-la-lee
I held her close and I asked her again
"If she was gonna be my baby?"
It felt so good when she answered me, "Oh yeah, oh yeah"
"Oh yeah, oh yeah, oh yeah"

Wanna know how my story ends?

Sha-la-la-la-lee, yeah

Well, we invited just a few close friends

Sha-la-la-la-lee, yeah

Sha-la-la-la-la-la-lee

Sha-la-la-la-la-la-lee

Sha-la-la-la-la-la-lee

Hey sha-la-la-la-la-la-lee, yeah

Sha-la-la-la-la-la-lee, yeah

Sing my song now, sha-la-la-la-la-la-la-lee, yeah

Hey, sha-la-la-la-la-la-la-la-la-lee, yeah

Come on, sha-la-la-la-la-la-la-lee, yeah

Help me out, sha-la-la-la-la-la-la-la-la-la-lee

(Sha-la-la-la-la-la-la-la-la-la-la-la-la-la-lee)

(Sha-la-la-la-la-la-la-la-la-la-la-la-la-la-lee)

Sha-la-la-la-la-la-lee

Sha-la-la-la-la-la-lee," sang Steve Marriott, ably backed up by fellow Small Faces bandmates, Ronnie Lane on bass guitar, Ian McLagan on keyboards, Kenney Jones on drums, with Steve Marriott also pulling things closely together on lead guitar.

The crowd went bonkers, and were screaming the place down, with elation and jubilation. The Small Faces had started the concert with a bang, and went straight into another track.

Chapter Two

The next song that was performed by The Small Faces was "You Need Loving". A track that was written by Steve Marriott and Ronnie Lane, which was always popular with the mod crowd, and was an album track on the L.P "Small Faces", which was released on 14th May 1966, and was their first L.P. It reached number 3 in the chart, spending 25 weeks there, and was recorded on the Decca label.

"Woah, I need foolin'
Hey woman, you need coolin'
I'm gonna send you right back to schoolin', alright
Make your way down the new side in your heart, woman
You know how woman
You need lovin' baby, yeah, lovin' alright
I know you need lovin' you hear
Oh yeah, alright
That's right, well, I've been yearnin'
Hey baby, you've been burnin'
We'll have a fun time, alright
You'll get some lovin' yeah
'Cause baby, we're gonna excite you
Deep in your heart woman
You need good lovin', yeah
Oh lovin', alright
That's all you need, lovin' baby
Yeah, alright
Eeny-meany-miney-mo
Eeny-meany-miney-mo
Can't take it no more
I can't monkey and I can't dog
Can't do the monkey, yeah
I said you know how to pony?
Mony baloney, I took you to the flyer
Passed me by
Oh, rock your pony

Mashed potato

Said I want to show you

I want to show you

It's alright, it's alright, yeah

Woman, you neeeeeeeeed looooooovin', yeaaaaaah, yeah," sang Steve Marriott forcibly, strongly, passionately and with a great blues tone. He was superbly backed up by his fellow Small Faces band members, Ronnie Lane, Kenney Jones and Ian McLagan.

"E Too D" was next. And this was another stomping good song, with a great beat, harmony and rhythm, and was also taken from the L.P. "Small Faces".

"Sometimes I feel like a frustrated child, alright

I got everything I want and there's nothing that I need

I can't stop my brain from running wild, oh no!

Running wild, my brain from running wild, alright

Sometimes I'm looking inside myself, and I don't like what I see

Seems like my soul is made of paper

So I took a look outside myself

Trying to get myself together

Things have changed now I find

I've just been messing, messing up my mind

So now my troubles are all over

And I'm pleased to find that I was right and they were wrong

I have messed up my mind

You see these colours? Hear those voices?

Something's burning

I can't take it no more," sang Steve Marriott, loudly, with expression, feeling and guts.

The Small Faces had really hit the zone, and were on cloud nine. They had performed admirably with their opening songs and were improving. They continued with "Hey Girl", a record that reached number 10 in the pop chart, and spent nine weeks there. It was their third single release and was available to buy from 12th May 1966, on Decca records.

"Girl, hold my hand (hand)
Girl, I know you'll understand (stand)
That I've been waiting
For a long long time
Think everything's
Gonna turn out fine
(Hey, hey) it's alright
(Hey, hey) it's alright
(Hey, hey) my, my, my
(Hey, hey) yeah, yeah, yeah
Girl, treat me kind (kind)
And girl, I think you'll find (find)
That no one can love you better than me
Close your eyes and I think you'll see
(Hey, hey) it's alright
(Hey, hey) my, my, my
(Hey, hey) come on children
(Hey, hey) my, oh, my
When I think of what I've missed
It makes me laugh inside
All the girls that I ain't kissed
Just to keep my pride
Yeah, yeah, yeah, yeah
So girl, look around (around)

And girl, see what we've found (found)
We've found something we can't fight
Don't think twice, it'll be alright, now
(Hey, hey) it's alright
(Hey, hey) I said, my, my, yeah
(Hey, hey) it's alright
(Hey, yeah) hey, yeah, it's alright
(Hey, hey) hey, hey
(Hey, yeah) hey yeah, it's alright
(Hey, ow) hey, ooh, it's alright
(Hey, ooh) hey, yeah, it's alright
(Hey, hey) c'mon, shake your hand
(Hey, hey) alright, a promised land
(Hey, hey) yeah, woh, it's alright
(Hey, hey) you know what I mean
It's alright

Well I say, alright, alright, alright," sang Steve Marriott on lead guitar and lead vocals, backed up by Kenney Jones on drums, Ronnie Lane on bass guitar and Ian McLagan on keyboards.

The music didn't stop and The Small Faces continued with "All or Nothing".

A track that was released on 11th August 1966, which reached number 1, and spent 12 weeks on the chart. And it was on the Decca label again.

"I thought you'd listen to my reasoning
But now I see you don't hear a thing
Try to make you see, how it's got to be
Yes, it's alright, (all or nothing)
Yeah, yeah, (all or nothing)

Come on, hot here
(All or nothing, for me)
Things could work out
Just like I want them to, yeah
If I could have the other half of you, yeah
You know I would, I can't
If only I could
Yes, it's yeah (all or nothing)
Oh yeah, (all or nothing)
You'll hear my children say
(All or nothing) for me
Ba-ba-ba-ba
Ba-ba-bad-a-ba
Ba-ba-ba-ba
Ba-ba-bad-a-ba
I didn't tell you no lies, yeah
So don't just sit there and cry, girl
Yeah, (all or nothing)
(All or nothing) (all or nothing)
Do you know what I mean? yeah?
You got to, got to, got to keep on tryin' yeah
(All or nothing) um, hum, yeah
(All or nothing) to keep on working out for me
(All or nothing) for me, for me, for me
Come on children, yeah
(All or nothing) yeah, yeah, yeah, yeah
(All or nothing) I keep on singing to myself
(All or nothing) yeah, for me, yeah," sang out Steve Marriott
loudly and assertively, with passion, soul and feeling, on lead

vocals and lead guitar, with Ronnie Lane on bass guitar, Kenney Jones on drums and Ian McLagan on keyboards.

"Thank you!" shouted Steve Marriott, as he left the stage with the other band members.

"Next up, is Swagger the mods. Yes, Swagger the mods are what we are calling them from now on, as there's another band called Swagger the rockers. So, here we have Swagger the mods!" called Roger Daltrey, still acting as the compere.

Swagger the mods came up on stage, and began with "A Groovy Kind Of Love", originally recorded by The Mindbenders, which was released on 13th January 1966, where it reached number 2 in the chart, and spent 14 weeks there. It was on the Fontana record label, and was written by Carole Bayer Sager and Toni Wine.

"When I'm feelin' blue
All I have to do
Is take a look at you
Then I'm not so blue
When you're close to me
I can feel your heart beat
I can hear you breathing
In my ear
Wouldn't you agree
Baby you and me
Got a groovy kind of love
(Groovy kind of love)
We got a groovy kind of love
(Groovy kind of love)
Any time you want to
You can turn me on to

Anything you want to
Any time at all
When I taste your lips
Oh, I start to shiver
Can't control
The quivering inside
Wouldn't you agree
Baby you and me
Got a groovy kind of love
(A groovy kind of love)
We got a groovy kind of love
Instrumental (guitar playing)
When I'm in your arms
Nothing seems to matter
If the world would shatter
I don't care
Wouldn't you agree
Baby you and me
Got a groovy kind of love
(A groovy kind of love)
We got a groovy kind of love
(Groovy kind of love)

We got a groovy kind of love," sang Ted on lead vocals and lead guitar, backed up by Sid on drums and Fred on bass guitar.

They didn't beat about the bush and moved on to the next song, and the cheering from the crowd was loud, vociferous and beautiful in the ears of Ted, Sid and Fred. They were ready to belt out "Hold Tight" next, which was originally recorded by Dave Dee, Dozy, Beaky, Mick and Tich, which charted at number 4 for 17 weeks, and was released on 3rd March 1966. It was on the Fontana record label, and proved popular with the mass of mods and rockers fans today.

"Hold tight, count to three
Gotta stay close by me
And hold tight, sing and shout
Just ride my round-a-bout
And hold tight, shut your eyes
Girl you suit me for
Si-ay-ay-ay-ize
Forget the other guys
You'll never fall, each time you call
Hold tight, hold tight, hold tight, tight, tight, tight, tight
Hold tight, make me feel
What you say is for real
And hold tight, carousel
Girl you'll soon ring my bell
And hold tight, we will fly
Swingin' low, swingin'
High-ay-ay-ay-ay
We're gonna make the sky
You'll never fall, each time you call
Hold tight, hold tight, hold tight, tight, tight, tight, tight
Guitar musical instrumental, with percussion
Hold tight, count to three
Gotta stay close by me
And hold tight, sing and shout
Just ride my round-a-bout
And hold tight, shut your eyes
Girl you suit me for
Si-ay-ay-ay-ize

Forget the other guys

You'll never fall, each time you call

Hold tight, hold tight, hold tight, tight, tight, tight, tight,

Guitar instrumental with percussion, to finish," played and sang Ted on lead vocals and lead guitar, ably backed up by Sid on harmonies and drums, and with Fred on bass guitar and harmonies. And it lifted the roof off the venue, as the noise was earth shattering and blaring, but with a distinct musical excellence.

Chapter Three

1966 was World Cup football year. England had qualified as host nation, and would be taking part in the tournament in the summer months of June and July.

On 5th January 1966, in a friendly match at Goodison Park, Liverpool, the home of Everton FC, in preparation for the forthcoming World Cup tournament, England played Poland, with close to 48,000 people in attendance. The England team that night was ;

1, goalkeeper, Gordon Banks, Leicester City

2, right full back defender, George Cohen, Fulham

3, left full back defender, Ray Wilson, Everton

4, midfielder, Nobby Stiles, Manchester United

5, central defender, Jack Charlton, Leeds United

6, central defender, Bobby Moore, West Ham United, (captain)

7, midfielder, Alan Ball, Blackpool

8, forward, Roger Hunt, Liverpool

9, centre forward, Joe Baker, Arsenal

10, inside forward, George Eastham, Arsenal

11, left winger, Gordon Harris, Burnley.

Every game between now and the World Cup tournament was going to be important.

The Polish team was as follows;

1, goalkeeper, Marian Szeja

2, defender, Jacek Gmoch

3, defender, Henryk Brejza

4, defender, Stanislaw Oslizlo

5, outside left, Andrzej Rewilak

6, midfielder, Piotr Suski

7, midfielder, Zygmunt Schmidt

8, inside right, Jan Wilim II

9, forward, Jozef Galeczka

10, forward, Jerzy Sadek

11, forward, Janusz Kowalik

12, substitute, Jan Banas, replaced Jan Wilim II in the 39th minute.

The score was 1-1, with Bobby Moore scoring in the 74th minute, replying to Jerzy Sadek's opening goal in the 43rd minute. It was a wet January night and a glue-pot pitch at Goodison Park, and Moore latched on to a pass from Leeds United defender Jack Charlton, following a quick move started by the Burnley winger Gordon Harris, who was deputising for the injured Bobby Charlton.

This was the first ever match between England and Poland and the first full international for 13 years at a Goodison ground that was to be one of the World Cup venues.

Incessant rain turned the pitch into a quagmire, that made every step a challenge. No doubt bouyed by his first England goal, only 2 was scored by Moore in 108 matches, the England captain stormed into the penalty area in the closing minutes to meet a centre from the tireless Alan Ball, and powered a header against the crossbar.

Alf Ramsey played a 4-3-3 with Stiles, Ball and Eastham working together in midfield. England wore white crew necked jerseys, blue shorts, and white socks. It was Alf Ramsey's 31st match in charge, and he had won 17, drew 8 and lost 6, with 76 goals scored for, and 45 goals scored against, Ramsey was appointed on 25th October 1962.

Poland wore red jerseys, red shorts, and white socks with red tops. Their manager was Ryszard Koncewicz. 48,000 soaked-through spectators witnessed England's first match of 1966, in this World Cup year.

The next match for England was against West Germany on 23rd February 1966, in another friendly. England's team on this occasion was;

1, goalkeeper, Gordon Banks, Leicester City

2, right full back defender, George Cohen, Fulham

3, left full back defender, Ray Wilson, Everton, injured in 42nd minute

12, substitute, Keith Newton, Blackburn Rovers, replaced Ray Wilson 42 minutes

4, centre half defender, Norman Hunter, Leeds United

5, centre half defender, Jack Charlton, Leeds United

6, centre half defender, Bobby Moore, West Ham United (captain)

7, midfielder, Alan Ball, Blackpool

8, midfielder, Nobby Stiles, Manchester United

9, midfielder/forward, Bobby Charlton, Manchester United

10, forward, Geoff Hurst, West Ham United

11, forward, Roger Hunt, Liverpool

The West Germany team was;

1, goalkeeper, Hans Tilkowski, Borussia Dortmund

2, defender, Friedel Lutz, Eintracht Frankfurt

3, midfielder, Max Lorenz, Werder Bremen

4, defender, Willi Schulz, SV Hamburger

5, defender, Wolfgang Weber, FC Koln

6, midfielder, Horst Szymaniak, Tasmania 1900 Berlin

7, midfielder, Werner Kramer, MSV Duisburg

8, defender, Franz Beckenbauer, Bayern Munich

9, forward, Sigfried Held, Borussia Dortmund

10, forward, Gunter Netzer, Borussia Monchengladbach

11, forward, Heinz Hornig, FC Koln, replaced in 44th minute by Alfred Heib

12, substitute, forward, Alfred Heib, 1860 Munich, replaced Heinz Hornig in 44th minute.

The venue was Wembley, with 75,000 spectators in attendance, and England won 1-0 with a Nobby Stiles goal. Roger Hunt's powerful header from George Cohen's cross was only parried by the West German goalkeeper, Hans Tilkowski, and Nobby Stiles was there to tap the ball into the net as he followed up the ricochet.

Gordon Banks was in fine form, making a number of crucial saves. And in the dying minutes of the game, West Germany had a goal disallowed following a linesman's decision that the ball had gone over the by-line. Geoff Hurst earned his first cap. Nobby Stiles scored his first England goal. And Keith Newton, coming on as a substitute for Ray Wilson also earned his first England cap. The weather wasn't great. It was another wet night. But at least England got a win, 1-0, to keep their 1966 unbeaten record intact, with the World Cup looming large, starting on 11th July 1966 until 30th July 1966. The next match for England in their preparations for the World Cup was the Home International game against Scotland.

England were playing in white crew neck jerseys, blue shorts and white socks. Scotland were in the Umbro playing kit of dark blue crew neck jerseys, white collars and cuffs, white shorts, blue socks with red tops. The attendance was 133,000 spectators, who had crammed, jam packed into the Hampden Park stadium, with a 3pm kick off. England were looking for their first win at Hampden Park since 1958, which was eight years without a win in Scotland, and the Scotland line up was as follows;

1, Bobby Ferguson, goalkeeper, Kilmarnock

2, John Greig, defender, Rangers

3, Tommy Gemmell, defender, Celtic

4, Bobby Murdoch, midfield, Celtic

5, Ronnie McKinnon, central defender, Rangers

6, Jimmy Baxter, central defender, Rangers

7, Jimmy Johnstone, right winger, Celtic

8, Denis Law, forward, Manchester United

9, William Wallace, forward, Hearts

10, Billy Bremner, midfield, Leeds United

11, Willy Johnston, left winger, Rangers

The Scotland manager was John Prentice, who had been appointed on 24th March 1966 and was also the manager of Clyde FC.

England's teamsheet was as follows;

1, Gordon Banks, goalkeeper, Leicester City

2, George Cohen, right full back defender, Fulham

3, Keith Newton, left full back defender, Blackburn Rovers

4, Nobby Stiles, midfield, Manchester United

5, Jack Charlton, central defender, Leeds United

6, Bobby Moore, central defender, West Ham United

7, Alan Ball, midfield, Blackpool

8, Roger Hunt, forward, Liverpool

9, Bobby Charlton, attacking midfield, Manchester United

10, Geoff Hurst, forward, West Ham United

11, John Connelly, winger, Manchester United

The England manager was Alf Ramsey, in his 33rd match as boss. The match was played at a frenetic, lightning fast pace, with plenty of tough, robust tackles and challenges flying in, throughout the game. But there was a whole host of defensive blunders by both teams.

Geoff Hurst scored his first goal for England in the 19th minute, to start the spree that excited the English fans in the vast 133,000 crowd. Roger Hunt added a second goal, before a superbly headed goal by Denis Law, who had been left unmarked, got one back for Scotland. It was a typical daredevil style header by Law, who threw himself forward, twisting and turning his head to secure great contact with the ball.

Roger Hunt was having a great match for England, showing silky skills and was on the mark again with another goal to make it 3-1. All three England goals were brilliant and clinical and found the net with power, and Hunt was sublime in his finishing, to poach, drive and shoot the ball into the net.

Celtic's Jimmy Johnstone was a man on fire, playing out of his skin, and he jinked, dribbled and skillfully prodded the ball home for a second Scottish goal, to make the score 3-2. But Bobby Charlton let fly with a thunderbolt shot through a maze of legs and bodies, leaving Bobby Ferguson the Scottish goalkeeper unsighted, and the ball flew into the back of the net to restore England's two goal lead. Bobby Charlton was unplayable, as he orchestrated the play in midfield, and was everywhere on the pitch.

Jimmy Johnstone then turned the England defence inside and out with a mazy, speedy run and scored a remarkable goal six minutes from the end, curling the ball into the goal which somehow deceived Gordon Banks.

This match had everything. Goals, passion, skill, pace, excitement and controversy. There should have been four penalties awarded. Two for either side. Stiles pulled Johnstone's shirt in the penalty area. Baxter handled the ball on the goal line. Bremner was fouled on the edge of the penalty area and Ball too was fouled inside the penalty box. But the referee didn't see any of them and the score remained 4-3.

It was looking good for England with only a few months to go before the World Cup started. Two wins and a draw was encouraging form for the Three Lions. The match was good to watch for the fans. But Alf Ramsey was not impressed. He said after the game, "There was some appalling football played out there," and "We must be tighter at the back." Wise words from the England boss, as he steered the ship forward to the next friendly.

England v Yugoslavia was the next match in the run up to the 1966 World Cup, and was played on 4th May 1966, at Wembley at 7 45pm. England lined up like this, in front of 55,000 spectators;

1, Gordon Banks, goalkeeper, Leicester City

2, Jimmy Armfield, right full back defender, Blackpool

3, Ray Wilson, left full back defender, Everton

4, Martin Peters, left midfield, West Ham United

5, Jack Charlton, central defender, Leeds United

6, Norman Hunter, central defender, Leeds United

7, Terry Paine, outside right winger, Southampton

8, Jimmy Greaves, forward, Tottenham Hotspur

9, Bobby Charlton, forward, Manchester United

10, Geoff Hurst, forward, West Ham United

11, Bobby Tambling, outside left winger, Chelsea

England wore white crew neck jerseys, blue shorts and white socks.

The Yugoslavia team was as follows;

1, Milutin Soskic, goalkeeper

2, Vinko Cuzzi, right full back defender

3, Zivorad Jevtic, left full back defender

4, Radoslav Becejac, midfield

5, Branko Rasovic, defender

6, Velibor Vasovic, midfield

7, Spasoje Samardzic, outside right wing

8, Dzemaludin Musovic, forward

9, Vojislav Melic, centre forward

10, Josip Skoblar, forward

11, Dragan Dzajic, outside left wing

The manager was Aleksander Tirnanic, and they played in blue crew neck jerseys, white shorts and red socks.

Jimmy Greaves returned to the England team, following his five months lay off with hepatitis, and he marked his come back with a 9th minute goal. Bobby Charlton scored another amazing screamer from long range, in the 34th minute, to wrap up an England victory, after being announced as the "Footballer Of The Year 1966." And he celebrated it in style, with a typical Charlton goal. Martin Peters, who Alf Ramsey described, as "being ten years ahead of his time," twice came close to marking his debut with a goal, against a highly skilled Yugoslavia side. It was England's last home game before the World Cup, and they responded with a strong all round performance, that sent a mood of optimism shooting through the country. England winning 2-0, meant it's an unbeaten 1966 so far, with the big prize of the World Cup only two months away.

Chapter Four

England had four friendlies arranged in the space of nine days, in an intense preparation for what was to come in the World Cup tournament, with a mini-tour of Scandinavia.

On 26th June 1966, England faced Finland away, and they lined up as follows;

1, Gordon Banks, goalkeeper, Leicester City
2, Jimmy Armfield, right full back defender, Blackpool, captain
3, Ray Wilson, left full back defender, Everton
4, Martin Peters, right half back midfield, West Ham United
5, Jack Charlton, centre half back defender, Leeds United
6, Norman Hunter, left half back defender, Leeds United
7, Ian Callaghan, outside right winger, Liverpool
8, Roger Hunt, inside right forward, Liverpool
9, Bobby Charlton, centre forward, Manchester United
10, Geoff Hurst, inside left forward, West Ham United
11, Alan Ball, outside left winger, Blackpool

England wore white crew necked shirts, blue shorts and white socks, which was the 1965/66 season Umbro home uniform. It was Jimmy Armfield's 15th and final captaincy.

Finland lined up as follows;

1, Martti Halme, goalkeeper
2, Pertti Makipaa, right full back
3, Rainer Aho, left full back
4, Timo Kautonen, right half back
5, Reijo Kanerva, centre half back
6, Seppo Kilponen, left half back
7, Markku Kumpulampi, outside right winger

8, Matti Makela, inside right forward

9, Markku Hyvarinen, centre forward

10, Aulis Laine, inside left forward

11, Antero Hyttinen, outside left winger

The captain was Matti Makela. The manager was Olavi Laaksonen. And Finland played in blue jerseys, white shorts and blue socks. The referee was Frede Hansen, and the match was played in Toolo, Helsinki, at 7 pm local time, 6 pm British Summer Time, with 12, 899 in attendance at the match.

Martin Peters scored his first England goal, opening the scoring, to give England a 1-0 lead. Alan Ball missed a penalty, in a game that will be remembered for the many missed chances, than those that were actually taken, by Roger Hunt, Martin Peters and Jack Charlton, which was a freak goal from a last minute shot from out on the byline. Ian Callaghan made an impressive debut alongside his Liverpool team mate Roger Hunt, as Alf Ramsey continued his experiment of playing with just one winger. Peters goal was timed at 42 minutes. Hunt scored in the 44th minute, with Charlton hitting the net in the 89th minute, to give England a comfortable 3-0 win. This was the first of a four game pre-World Cup tour, played on Sunday 26th June 1966.

England's next match was against Norway on Wednesday 29th June 1966. England's teamsheet was as follows;

1, Ron Springett, goalkeeper, Sheffield Wednesday

2, George Cohen, right full back, Fulham

3, Gerry Byrne, left full back, Liverpool

4, Nobby Stiles, midfield, Manchester United

5, Ron Flowers, centre half, Wolves

6, Bobby Moore, left half back defender, West Ham United captain

7, Terry Paine, outside right, Southampton

8, Jimmy Greaves, inside right forward, Tottenham Hotspur

9, Bobby Charlton, centre forward, Manchester United

10, Roger Hunt, inside left forward, Liverpool

11, John Connelly, outside left, Manchester United

England wore white crew necked shirts, blue shorts and white socks. The 1965/66 season Umbro home uniform. Bobby Moore captained the side, which was his 22nd captaincy at just 25 years old. Alf Ramsey was the manager, in his 36th match as boss. It was goalkeeper Ron Springett's final England appearance, along with Gerry Byrne's last England match, and it was also Ron Flowers final game for the Three Lions of England. Springett had served England from 1959 to 1966, earning 33 caps, in 7 years. Byrne had played for England from 1963 to 1966, picking up 2 caps and scoring 0 goals in three years. And Ron Flowers had served England from 1955 till 1966, earning 49 caps and scoring 10 goals in 11 years.

Jimmy Greaves scored a record sixth hat trick, and extended his record as top goalscorer for England, up to the present 1966 season, and he also became the record goal scorer of friendly goals. His third goal in this match equalled the record of 18 held by Tom Finney, followed by his fourth which broke the record. Ron Springett extended his record of being England's most capped goalkeeper up to the 1966 season.

The Norway team lined up as follows;

1, Sverre Andersen, goalkeeper

2, Roar Johansen, right full back

3, Arild Mathisen, left full back

4, Arne Pedersen, right half back

5, Finn Thorsen, centre half defender

6, Edgar Stakset, left half back

7, Harald Sunde, outside right

8, Ole Stavrum, inside right

9, Harald Berg, centre forward

10, Olav Nilsen, inside left

11, Erik Johansen, outside left

Norway played in red jerseys, white shorts and blue socks. The game was played at the Ullevaal stadium in Ullevaal in Oslo, kicking off at 7 pm local time, with 34,000 spectators in attendance. The referee was Hans Carlsson, with the linesmen being Folke Johansson and Curt Liedberg.

Jimmy Greaves scored four goals for the second time in his international career, against a Norwegian team that was out of its depth. A misplaced back pass by Ron Flowers gifted Norway a fourth minute lead, when Harald Sunde capitalised on the error, to slot the ball past goalkeeper Ron Springett. But after that initial shock, it was England that took the game by the scruff of the neck, and they totally dominated play, winning the match 6-1. Greaves scored all of his goals in the first half, and was now England's top goal scorer, with 43 goals from 49 international matches. Bobby Moore got on the scoresheet with a twenty-five yard drive, that could have come from the boot of Bobby Charlton, who created the sixth goal for John Connelly, in a second half played at exhibition pace.

Football Association and Chelsea chairman Joe Mears, a long-time friend and supporter of Jimmy Greaves, died of a heart attack in Oslo the day after the match, which cast a feeling of dark despair over the entire England squad. Mears, "Mr Chelsea", had been the driving force in the preparation of England's hosting of the World Cup finals. It was tough, but

England needed to soldier on. Their World Cup chances depended on it. And the squad led by Alf Ramsey closed ranks tightly, and pledged to the nation that they would give everything they had, to win the World Cup, in the memory and respect of "Mr Chelsea", Joe Mears.

But there was the small matter of two further friendlies still to complete, and the mini four game Scandinavia tour continued in earnest, with England's next match against Denmark. After three days off, the game took place on Sunday 3rd July 1966, and was played at the Idraetsparken stadium, Copenhagen.

Peter Bonetti played in goal, and earned his first cap. It was Jimmy Greaves 50th cap, and George Eastman's last cap. Jack Charlton scored England's 1150th goal.

England lined up like this;

1, Peter Bonetti, Chelsea, goalkeeper

2, George Cohen, Fulham, right full back

3, Ray Wilson, Everton, left full back

4, Nobby Stiles, Manchester United, midfield

5, Jack Charlton, Leeds United, central defender

6, Bobby Moore, West Ham United, central defender, captain

7, Alan Ball, Blackpool, midfield

8, Jimmy Greaves, Tottenham Hotspur, inside right forward

9, Geoff Hurst, West Ham United, centre forward

10, George Eastham, Arsenal, inside left forward

11, John Connelly, Manchester United, outside left winger

England wore white crew necked jerseys, blue shorts and white socks, with black armbands in respect of the sudden death of "Mr Chelsea" and FA Chairman Joe Mears, who had passed away the day after the match against Norway.

Denmark lined up as follows;

1, Leif Nielsen, goalkeeper

2, Johnny Hansen, right full back

3, Leif Hartwig, left full back

4, John Petersen, right half

5, Henning Boel, centre half

6, Niels Moller, left half

7, Bent Schmidt, outside right winger

8, John Steen Olsen, inside right forward

9, Henning Enoksen, centre forward

10, Tom Sondergaard, inside left forward

11, Ulrik Le Fevre, outside left wing

Denmark wore red jerseys, white shorts, with red socks.

Jack Charlton and George Eastham scored the goals that gave England their sixth successive victory. Peter Bonetti, the Chelsea goalkeeper made his first appearance for England and performed very well, on a bumpy, uneven pitch, which led to many errors being made in front of him. The amateurs of Denmark, playing for pride, were tough, rough and robust in their challenges, which brought about a competitive edge, that made the game very physical, and brought out the nasty side in England's midfield warriors, Nobby Stiles and Alan Ball, who were severely lectured on numerous occasions by the Canadian referee. On another day, there may have been several red cards flashed for foul play. Jimmy Greaves the four goal hero in the previous game, hardly touched the ball in his 50th international, and the final score was England 2 Denmark 0.

The final match on this pre-world cup tour, was against Poland, at 6 pm, on 5th July 1966, played at the Slaski stadium in Katowice, Chorzow, in front of 90,000 spectators.

England wore red crew necked jerseys, white shorts and red socks, and lined up as follows;

1, Gordon Banks, goalkeeper, Leicester City   1, Marian Szeja, goalkeeper

2, George Cohen, right back, Fulham   2, Roman Strzalkowski, right back

3, Ray Wilson, left back, Everton   3, Henryk Brejza, left back

4, Nobby Stiles, midfield, Manchester United   4, Zygmunt Anczok, midfield

5, Jack Charlton, centre half, Leeds United   5, Walter Winkler, centre half

6, Bobby Moore, left half back, West Ham United   6, Jacek Gmoch, left half

7, Alan Ball, midfield, Blackpool   7, Piotr Suski, midfield

8, Jimmy Greaves, forward, Tottenham Hotspur   8, Jozef Galeczka, forward

9, Bobby Charlton, centre forward, Manchester United   9, Wlodzimierz Lunanski

10, Roger Hunt, forward, Liverpool   10, Jan Liberda, forward

11, Martin Peters, midfield, West Ham United   11, Janusz Kowalik, midfield

Poland wore white jerseys, red shorts and white socks.

Roger Hunt scored a magnificent goal in the 13th minute, to give England a 1-0 win, in this final match before the World Cup finals. It was England's seventh successive victory, which was capped by the unveiling of the new formation that Alf Ramsey had created, *playing without wingers*, in what the England boss reckoned was his best eleven. This team would go on to better things. But for now they were happy to go unbeaten in 1966, with the World Cup only days away.

Chapter Five

Swagger the mods, alongside Swagger the rockers, with The Who, The Small Faces, The Kinks and the Rolling Stones, had continued with their 1966 World Tour, and after the New Year's success in Kenya, they moved to Pretoria in South Africa. Pretoria welcomed the mods and rockers cultures with open arms, mixing together on scooters for the mods, with their parkas, and motorbikes for the rockers, with their leather jackets. The African mods and rockers really got down to the business, and loved their music in 1966.

Whilst football fever was bubbling across the globe, for the forthcoming World Cup in England, music fever was bubbling up in Africa, with the top groups of the day taking time to bring unity, peace and love across the planet. There was no segregation with music. There was no politics in music. There was no vice, no trouble, nor moneymaking scams or hatred with music. Just the good old love of having a great vibe, great time, and a great party feeling, engaging everyone.

Pretoria is one of South Africa's three capital cities, serving as the seat of the executive branch of government, and as hosts to all foreign embassies to South Africa. Pretoria straddles the Apies River and extends eastward into the foothills of the Magaliesberg Mountains. The Afrikaans pronunciation is Pre-tuaria. It has a reputation as an academic city and centre of research being home to the Tshware University of Technology.

These students were the gig going guests at the mods and rockers concerts, and had welcomed the artists performing their brand of fine music, with open arms. Pretoria was founded in 1855 by Marthinus Pretorius, a leader of the Voortrekkers, who named it after his father, Andries Pretorius, and chose a spot on the banks of the Apies River, (Afrikaans for Monkey's River) to be the new capital of the South African Republic (Dutch; Zuid Afrikaansche Republiek ZAR)

The elder Pretorius had become a national hero of the Voortrekkers after his victory over the Dingane and Zulus in the "Battle of Blood River" in 1838.

The elder Pretorius had also negotiated the Sand River Convention in 1852, in which the United Kingdom acknowledged the independence of the Transvaal. It became capital of the South Africa Republic on 1st May 1860. The founding of Pretoria as the capital of South Africa Republic marked the end of the Boers movements of the Great Trek.

Pretoria was nicknamed "Jacaranda City" because of the thousands of jacaranda trees that were planted along its streets, parks and gardens. There were 50,000 jacarandas that lit up the area, and they looked beautiful.

Purple is a colour that is often associated with the city, and is included on the local council logos and services, and the jacaranda trees didn't disappoint, as they were bursting with glorious colour, as the crowds flocked to the gig at the 51,000 capacity Loftus Versfeld Stadium, which was located in the Arcadia suburb of Pretoria in the Gauteng province, at 440 Kirkness Street, which was usually used for rugby union and football.

Starting the gig was The Who, with the song "Substitute" which was released on the Reaction record label on 10th March 1966, and it reached as high as number 5 in the chart, spending a total of 13 weeks there.

"You think we look pretty good together
You think my shoes are made of leather
But I'm a substitute for another guy
I look pretty tall but my heels are high
The simple things you see are all complicated
I look pretty young, but I'm just back-dated yeah
(Substitute) your lies for fact
(Substitute) I see right through your plastic mac
(Substitute) I look all white, but my dad was black
(Substitute) my fine linen suit is really made out of sack
I was born with a plastic spoon in my mouth
The north side of my town faced east and the east was facing south
And now you dare to look me in the eye
Those crocodile tears are what you cry
It's a genuine problem, you won't try
To work it out at all you just pass it by, pass it by
(Substitute) me for him
(Substitute) my coke for gin
(Substitute) you for my mum
(Substitute) at least I'll get my washing done
I'm a substitute for another guy
I look pretty tall but my heels are high
The simple things you see are all complicated
I look pretty young, but I'm just back-dated yeah
I was born with a plastic spoon in my mouth

The north side of my town faced east and the east was facing south
And now you dare to look me in the eye
Those crocodile tears are what you cry
It's a genuine problem, you won't try
To work it out at all you just pass it by, pass it by
(Substitute) me for him
(Substitute) my coke for gin
(Substitute) you for my mum
(Substitute) at least I'll get my washing done
(Substitute) your lies for fact
(Substitute) I see right through your plastic mac
(Substitute) I look all white but my dad was black
(Substitute) my fine looking suit is really made out of sack," belted out Roger Daltrey on lead vocals, ably backed up by Pete Townshend on lead guitar and backing vocals, Keith Moon on drums and John Entwistle on bass guitar and backing vocals.

The Pretorians in the audience screamed, stomped, shouted, cheered and applauded with delight. The Who had began the concert in style and they followed this one up with a second track, "I'm a Boy" which was released on 1st September 1966, on Reaction Records and reached number 2, charting for 13 weeks and was their fifth top ten hit.

"One little girl was called Jean-Marie
Another little girl was called Felicity
Another little girl was Sally-Joy
The other was me
And I'm a boy
My name is Bill and I'm a head case
They practice making-up on my face

Yeah, I feel lucky if I get trousers to wear
Spend days just taking hairpins from my hair
I'm a boy, I'm a boy
But my ma won't admit it
I'm a boy, I'm a boy
But if I say I am, I get it
Put your frock on, Jean-Marie
Plait your hair Felicity
Paint your nails, little Sally-Joy
Put this wig on little boy
I'm a boy, I'm a boy
But my ma won't admit it
I'm a boy, I'm a boy
But if I say I am, I get it
I wanna play cricket on the green
Ride my bike across the street
Cut myself and see my blood
I wanna come home all covered in mud
I'm a boy, I'm a boy
But my ma won't admit it
I'm a boy, I'm a boy
I'm a boy
I'm a boy, I'm a boy
I'm a boy, I'm a boy, I'm a boy
I'm a Boy, I'm a Boy!" sang Roger Daltrey on lead vocals, ably
backed up on backing vocals and lead guitar by Pete Townshend,
with Keith Moon on drums and John Entwistle on bass guitar and
vocal backing.

The roof was lifted by the noise in the 50,000 strong crowd, as they watched from the stands in the rugby union and football stadium. The Who had gone down very well.

Now it was time for The Kinks with "Sunny Afternoon", which reached number one, their third number one chart topper, and it was released on the Pye record label, and charted for 13 weeks, following its release on 9th June 1966.

"The taxman's taken all my dough
And left me in my stately home
Lazin' on a sunny afternoon
And I can't sail my yacht
He's taken everything I got
All I've got's this sunny afternoon
Save me, save me, save me from this squeeze
I got a big fat mama tryna break me
And I love to live so pleasantly
Live this life of luxury
Lazin' on a sunny afternoon
In the summertime
In the summertime
In the summertime
My girlfriend's run off with my car
And gone back to her ma and pa
Tellin' tales of drunkenness and cruelty
Now I'm sittin' here
Sippin' on my ice cold beer
Lazin' on a sunny afternoon
Help me, help me, help me
Sail away
Well, give me two good reasons why I oughta stay

'Cause I love to live so pleasantly
Live this life of luxury
Lazin' on a sunny afternoon
In the summertime
In the summertime
In the summertime
Oh save me, save me, save me from this squeeze
I got a big fat mama tryna break me
And I love to live so pleasantly
Live this life of luxury
Lazin' on a sunny afternoon
In the summertime
In the summertime
In the summertime
In the summertime

In the summertime," sang lead singer Ray Davies on rhythm guitar, with his brother Dave Davies on backing vocals and lead guitar, and Mick Avory on the drums.

The audience went wild with delight and applauded, cheered, screamed and roared their approval.

Chapter Six

After Pretoria, the entourage jetted off to Johannesburg, South Africa's biggest city and the capital of the Gauteng province. It began as a 19th century gold-mining settlement. Its sprawling Soweto township was once the home to Nelson Mandela and Desmond Tutu. Mandela's former residence is now the Mandela House Museum. Other Soweto museums that recount the struggle to end segregation include the sombre

Apartheid Museum and Constitution Hill, a former prison complex. Johnannesburg is informally known as Jozi, Joburg or "The City of Gold", and is classed as a mega city, and one of the 100 largest urban areas in the world.

The Johannesburg-Pretoria urban area, because of its strong links in transport making commuting feasible, is the 26th largest in the world, with 14 million inhabitants. It is the provincial capital and largest city of Gauteng, which is the wealthiest province in South Africa. Johannesburg is the seat of the Constitution Court, the highest court in South Africa. Most of the major South African companies and banks have their head offices in Johannesburg, and the city is located in the mineral rich Witwatersrand, (meaning "ridge of white waters" in Afrikaans) range of hills, and is the centre of a large scale gold and diamond trade. It was one of the host cities of the official tournament of the 2010 FIFA World Cup, and hosted the World Cup final. So, football has been ingrained into the life of the South African people for decades. The first language of Johnannesburg is Zulu, at 23%, and English at 20%, with Sesotho at 9.6%.

Gold was discovered in 1886 and the city of Johannesburg was born, on what had been a farm. Due to the extremely large gold deposit found along the Witwatersrand, within ten years the population had grown to 100,000 inhabitants. A separate city was created from the 1970's to the 1990's, known as Soweto, which is now part of Johannesburg. Soweto was an acronym for "Southern-western Townships" and originated as a collection of settlements on the outskirts of Johannesburg, populated by mainly native African workers from the gold mining industry. Soweto had been separated as a residential area for blacks only, with no whites allowed, with the blacks not permitted to live in the other white designated suburbs of Johannesburg. Lenasia was predominantly populated by English speaking South Africans of Indian descent. These areas too were designed as non-white zones, in accordance with the segregation policies of the South African government, and was known as apartheid.

The Kinks opened the show at Johannesburg's Rand Africaans University, (RAU) following the new rules. The British had controlled South Africa since 1900 and in 1966, South Africa broke free independently with the newly elected National Party, seeking to provide education in the Afrikaans language, as it had been in English up until this point. But the apartheid was still evident, with whites being kept separate from the blacks. However, these gigs broke free, in a hush-hush way, as the students bent the rules and mixed, black with white, and white with black. Nobody was any wiser. The lights were dimmed. The crowds were packed in and there were no law enforcers, such as the police or bouncers or politicians anywhere to be seen, so it was safe for the Soweto people to mix with those from Johannesburg, and enjoy the music together, in harmony. As free as a bird.

The Kinks began with "Dedicated Follower of Fashion", which was released on the Pye record label on 3rd March 1966, and reached number 4. It spent 11 weeks in the chart. The crowd loved this track and went wild with elation as the song began.

"They seek him here
They seek him there
His clothes are loud
But never square
It will make or break him, so he's got to buy the best

'Cause he's a dedicated follower of fashion
And when he does his little rounds
Round the boutiques of London town
Eagerly pursuing all the latest fads and trends
'Cause he's a dedicated follower of fashion
Oh yes he is (Oh yes he is)
Oh yes he is (Oh yes he is)
He thinks he's a flower to be looked at
And when he pulls his frilly nylon panties right up tight
He feels a dedicated follower of fashion
Oh yes he is (Oh yes he is)
Oh yes he is (Oh yes he is)
There's one thing that he loves and that is flattery
One week he's in polka-dots, the next week he's in stripes
'Cause he's a dedicated follower of fashion
They seek him here
They seek him there
In Regent Street
And Leicester Square
Everywhere the Carnabetian army marches on
Each one a dedicated follower of fashion
Oh yes he is (Oh yes he is)
Oh yes he is (Oh yes he is)
His world is built round discotheques and parties
This pleasure-seeking individual always looks his best
'Cause he's a dedicated follower of fashion
Oh yes he is (Oh yes he is)
Oh yes he is (Oh yes he is)
He flits from shop to shop
Just like a butterfly

In matters of the cloth he is as fickle as can be
'Cause he's a dedicated follower of fashion
He's a dedicated follower of fashion
He's a dedicated follower of fashion," belted out Ray Davies on lead vocals and rhythm guitar, who also wrote the song, and was ably backed up by his brother Dave Davies on lead guitar and backing vocals, with John Dalton on bass guitar and backing vocals, replacing the injured Pete Quaife, who had been injured in a car crash, and Mick Avory on the drums.

The go-go dancers were in great form, consisting of the gorgeous beauty contestants from Miss Hull, Jilly Jacobs, Jackie Jones, Rosie Wright, Becky Bright, Erica Shaw and Lily Lewis, dressed in white bikinis and looking hot, lush and sexy. They jived, grinded, hustled, shuffled and moved artistically and energetically in time to the Kinks music.

The Kinks left the stage to a rousing, superb, loud and vociferous cheer of approval from the crowd, for their opening number and the band continued with a second song, as an encore. They couldn't leave the stage. The crowd wanted another one of their musical masterpieces, and they performed "Tired Of Waiting For You", a record released on 21st January 1965, which reached number 1, and spent ten weeks on the chart. It was released on the Pye record label.

"So tired, tired of waiting
Tired of waiting for you
So tired, tired of waiting
Tired of waiting for you
I was a lonely soul
I had nobody 'till I met you
But you keep-a me waiting

All of the time
What can I do?
It's your life
And you can do what you want
Do what you like
But please don't keep-a me waiting
Please don't keep- a me waiting
'Cause I'm so tired, tired of waiting
Tired of waiting for you
So tired, tired of waiting
Tired of waiting for you
I was a lonely soul
I had nobody 'till I met you
But you keep-a me waiting
All of the time
What can I do?
It's your life
And you can do what you want
Do what you like
But please don't keep-a me waiting
Please don't keep-a me waiting
'Cause I'm so tired, tired of waiting
Tired of waiting for you
So tired, tired of waiting
Tired of waiting for you
For you

For you," sang Ray Davies on lead vocals and rhythm guitar, ably assisted by Mick Avory on drums, with Dave Davies on lead guitar and backing vocals, and John Dalton on bass guitar and backing vocals.

The Rolling Stones came on to the stage, as The Kinks left it, and the reception was fantastic. Not only was The Kinks cheered for their two tracks, but the Johannesburg people roared their approval for The Rolling Stones. The concert was living up to expectations. The Kinks were great. They sounded brilliant and the crowd appreciated them.

The go-go dancers slipped into something different, swapping bikinis for mini skirts and tee shirts, with no bra. What a sight that was to see.

The Rolling Stones got off to a quick start and began with "Get Off My Cloud", released on Decca records, on 28th October 1965, and reaching number one. It charted for 12 weeks.

"I live in an apartment
On the ninety-ninth floor of my block
And I sit at home looking out of the window
Imagining the world has stopped
Then in flies a guy
Who's all dressed up like a Union Jack
And says, "I've won five pounds if I have this kind of detergent pack"
I say hey (hey), you (you)
Get off of my cloud
Hey (hey), you (you)
Get off of my cloud
Hey (hey), you (you)
Get off of my cloud
Don't hang around 'cause two's a crowd
On my cloud, baby
The telephone is ringing
I say hi, it's me

Who is there on the line?

A voice says, hi, hello, how are you?

Well I guess I'm doing fine

He says, It's three am there's too much noise

Don't you people ever want to go to bed?

Just 'cause you feel so good, do you have to drive me out of my head?

I say hey (hey), you (you)

Get off of my cloud

Hey (hey), you (you)

Get off of my cloud

Hey (hey), you (you)

Get off of my cloud

Don't hang around 'cause two's a crowd

On my cloud, baby, yeah

I was sick and tired, fed up with this

And decided to take a drive downtown

It was so very quiet and peaceful

There was nobody, not a soul around

I laid myself out, I was so tired

And I started to dream

In the morning, the parking tickets were just like a flag

Stuck on my windscreen

I said hey (hey), you (you)

Get off of my cloud

Hey (hey), you (you)

Get off of my cloud

Hey (hey), you (you)

Get off of my cloud

Don't hang around, 'cause two's a crowd

On my cloud, baby

Hey (hey), you (you)

Get off of my cloud

Hey (hey), you (you)

Get off of my cloud

Hey (hey), you (you)

Get off of my cloud

Don't hang around, 'cause two's a crowd

So I say hey (hey), you (you)," sang Mick Jagger on lead vocals, assisted by Keith Richard on backing vocals and lead guitar, Brian Jones on slide guitar and rhythm guitar, weaving the instrument with Keith Richard, Bill Wyman on bass guitar and Charlie Watts on drums.

The crowd went wild, lifting the roof off the university building, with a terrific burst of energy and adulation. The Rolling Stones followed this one up with another and the crowd loved it. The beat was great. The sound was fantastic. The lighting was amazing, and the atmosphere was electric. The apartheid was totally forgotten, as Johannesburg came together with Soweto, in love and harmony.

Chapter Seven

The Rolling Stones invited Swagger the mods to join them on the stage in their next number, "Paint it Black". This record reached number one and was released on 19th May 1966, where it charted for 10 weeks, and was recorded on the Decca label.

The mods and rockers in the crowd howled their appreciation, as the Rolling Stones and Swagger the mods worked in tandem on the stage, with precision, as if they had been doing this all of their lives. They were smashing it.

"I see a red door
And I want it painted black
No colours anymore
I want them to turn black
I see the girls walk by
Dressed in their summer clothes
I have to turn my head
Until my darkness goes
I see a line of cars
And they're all painted black
With flowers and my love
Both never to come to come back
I've seen people turn their heads
And quickly look away
Like a newborn baby
It just happens everyday
I look inside myself
And see my heart is black
I see my red door
I must have it painted black
Maybe then, I'll fade away
And not have to face the facts
It's not easy facing up
When your whole world is black
No more will my green sea
Go turn a deeper blue
I could not foresee this thing
Happening to you

If I look hard enough
Into the setting sun
My love will laugh with me
Before the morning comes
I see a red door
And I want it painted black
No colours anymore
I want them to turn black
I see the girls walk by
Dressed in their summer clothes
I have to turn my head
Until my darkness goes
I wanna see it painted
Painted black
Black as night
Black as coal
I wanna see the sun
Blotted out from the sky
I wanna see it painted
Painted painted

Painted black, yeah," sang Mick Jagger and Ted as joint lead vocals, with Bill Wyman on bass guitar, along with Fred on bass guitar, Charlie Watts and Sid on drums, and Keith Richard on lead guitar with backing vocals, along with Brian Jones on rhythm guitar, holding it all together with style, aplomb and efficiency, and also playing the sitar and acoustic guitar, with Bill Wyman on the Hammond organ, to create a wall of sound, that echoed fabulously around the university arena, and was an experience for everyone in there.

The Rolling Stones left the stage and Swagger the mods stayed there, for it was their turn to perform on their own. They had done a great job working with the Rolling Stones and the crowd went wild. The dancers were gyrating, dressed in their skimpy mini skirts and tee shirts, with their braless boobs bouncing like footballs underneath the cotton fabric. The crowd was wowed by both the group Swagger the mods and the lush go-go dancers. The air was warm, the sweat was pouring down the bodies of the gyrating dancers, as they moved in time to the music, giving their all. Swagger the mods were performing The Miracles song, "Going to a Go-Go", which was highly appropriate, for the manner in which the go-go dancers were performing. They were certainly "going to a go-go!" This song was released on the Tamla Motown record label on 24th February 1966, reaching number 44 in the chart, where it spent 5 weeks there.

"Well there's a brand new place I've founda
Where people go from miles arounda
They come from everywhere and if you drop in there
You might see anyone in towna
Going to a go-go
(Everybody's) going to a go-go (come on now)
Don't you want to go (yeah)
A-one more time-yeah!
I'm going to a go-go, oh oh weee
Going to a go-go (baby come on now)
It doesn't matter where you are
A go-go can't be far
You'll see the people from your block
And don't be shocked
If you see your favourite star

Going to a go-go

('Cause everybody's)

Going to a go-go

(Oh come on now)

Don't you want to go

(Yeah people come on)

Na na na na na yeah

Tell me, don't you want to go

Yeah now it's alright

I'm going to a go-go

Yes I am

Going to a go-go

Oh come on now

It doesn't matter if the people stagger

It doesn't matter if you go dragger

You're sure to have some fun

I'm telling everyone

Most every taxi that you flag is

Going to a go-go

(Oh come on baby)

Going to a go-go

(Baby come on now)

Don't you want to go

(Yeah)

One more time, yeah

I'm going to a go-go

Oh oh whee

Going to a go-go

(Baby come on now)

Going to a go-go

(Come on baby)

Going to a go-go

Oh come on now

Going to a go-go," sang Ted on lead vocals and lead guitar, backed up by Sid on drums and backing vocals, and Fred on bass guitar with vocal backing. The crowd erupted into fits of hysteria and passion, as they loved that Motown sound, and they loved Swagger the mods.

The go-go dancers nipped off the stage, as they were burning up and needed to take a liquid refreshment and change their clothing again, reverting back to bikinis. It was too warm for the tee shirts and mini skirts. They reappeared in gold coloured two-piece bikinis, which looked very fetching and bright.

Swagger the mods started their second song, "This Old Heart Of Mine", which was an Isley Brothers track, that was released on 28th April 1966, and reached number 3, and was on the Tamla Motown record label, charting for a huge 17 weeks.

"This old heart of mine been broke a thousand times

Each time you break away

I fear you've gone to stay

Lonely nights that come

Memories that flow, bringing you back again

Hurting me more and more

Maybe it's my mistake to show this love I feel inside

'Cause each day that passes by, you got me

Never knowing , if I'm coming or going, but I, I love you

This old heart darling, is weak for you

I love you, yes I do, yes I do

These old arms of mine miss having you around

Make these tears inside

Start a-falling down
Always with half a kiss
You remind me of what I miss
Though I try to control myself
Like a fool I start grinning 'cause my head starts spinnin'
'Cause I,
I love you
This old heart, darling is weak for you
I love you, yes I do, yes I do
Ohh I try hard to hide, my hurt inside
This old heart of mine, always keeps me cryin'
The way you're treating me, leaves me incomplete
You're here for the day, gone for the week, now
But if you leave me a hundred times
A hundred times I'll take you back
I'm yours whenever you want me
I'm not too proud to shout it, tell the world about it
'Cause I,
I love you
This old heart darlin' is weak for you
I love you
This old heart darlin' is weak for you
I love you
This old heart darlin' is weak for you
I love you, yes I do, yes I do
I love you, yes I do, darling, is weak for you," sang Ted on lead vocals and lead guitar, backed up superbly by Fred on bass guitar and backing vocals, and Sid on drums and backing vocals.
The crowd went bananas. The elation was tremendous and Swagger the mods appreciated it. It made them want to do

better in the next song, which was a cover version of Manfred Mann's classic tune, "Pretty Flamingo", which reached number one, charted for 12 weeks, was on the HMV POP record label, and was released on 21st April 1966.

"On our block, all of the guys call her flamingo
'Cause her hair glows like the sun
And her eyes can light the skies
When she walks, she moves so fine like a flamingo
Crimson dress that clings so tight
She's out of reach and out of sight
When she walks by, she brightens up the neighbourhood
Oh every guy would make her his
If he just could, if she just would
Some sweet day, I'll make her mine pretty flamingo
Then every guy will envy me
'Cause paradise is where I'll be
Sha la la la la la la pretty flamingo
Sha la la la la la la pretty flamingo
When she walks by
She brightens up the neighbourhood
Oh every guy would make her his
If he just could, ha, if she just would
Some sweet day, I'll make her mine pretty flamingo
Then every guy will envy me
'Cause paradise is where I'll be
Sha la la la la la la pretty flamingo
Some day I'll make her mine
Yes I will
Yes I will

Sha la la la la la la pretty flamingo," sang Ted on lead vocals and lead guitar and ably backed up by Sid on drums and backing vocals and Fred on bass guitar.

Chapter Eight

Swagger the mods left the stage and were replaced instantly by Swagger the rockers. The crowd were continuing to cheer Swagger the mods for their previous number, "Pretty Flamingo", and the cheering intensified as Swagger the rockers began their first song, "I Feel Free", a Cream number, released on 15th December 1966 on Reaction Records, and reaching number 11 in the chart, where it spent 12 weeks. It was a favourite of the rockers in the audience and the mods enjoyed it too.

"Bomp, bomp, bomp, bomp, bomp, bomp
Bomp, bomp, bomp, bomp, bomp, bomp
I feel free
Bomp, bomp, bomp, bomp, bomp, bomp
I feel free
Bomp, bomp, bomp, bomp, bomp, bomp
I feel free
Bomp, bomp, bomp, bomp, bomp, bomp
I feel free
Bomp, bomp, bomp, bomp, bomp, bomp
I feel free
Bomp, bomp, bomp, bomp, bomp, bomp
I feel free
Bomp, bomp, bomp, bomp, bomp, bomp
I feel free
Bomp, bomp, bomp, bomp, bomp, bomp

I feel free

Bomp, bomp, bomp, bomp, bomp, bomp

I feel free

Feel when I dance with you

We move like the sea

You you're all I want to know

I feel free

I feel free

I feel free

I can walk down the street

There's no one there

Though the pavements are one huge crowd

I can drive down the road my eyes don't see

Though my mind wants to cry out loud

I, I, I, I, feel free

I feel free

I feel free

I can walk down the street

There's no one there

Though the pavements are one huge crowd

I can drive down the road my eyes don't see

Though my mind wants to cry out loud

Though my mind wants to cry out loud

Dance floor is like the sea

Ceiling is the sky

You're the sun and as you shine on me

I feel free

I feel free

I feel free

I, I, I, I, feel free," sang Rob Rule on lead vocals and lead guitar, Rick Prentiss on bass guitar and backing vocals, and Cyril Platt on drums, in a melodic, tight, excellent performance, which went down well with the Johannesburg crowd, who wailed, cheered, applauded, screamed and roared their approval.

Swagger the rockers went straight onto another song, "Wild Thing", which was a hit for The Troggs, that reached number 2 in the chart, where it spent 12 weeks, and was released on the Fontana record label, on 5th May 1966.

"Wild thing

You make my heart sing

You make everything groovy

Wild thing

Wild thing, I think I love you

But I wanna know for sure

Come on, hold me tight

I love you

Instrumental

Wild thing

You make my heart sing

You make everything groovy

Wild thing

Ocarina solo

Wild thing, I think you move me

But I wanna know for sure

So come on hold me tight

You move me

Wild thing

You make my heart sing

You make everything groovy

Wild thing

Oh, come on, wild thing

Check it, check it, wild thing," sang Rob Rule strongly, on lead vocals and lead guitar, Rick Prentiss on bass guitar, backing vocals and ocarina flute and Cyril Platt on drums and backing vocals. The crowd went wild.

Next up was "Shotgun Wedding", a song performed originally by Roy C. It was released on 21st April 1966 on Island Records, where it reached number 6 and charted for 11 weeks.

"People were standing, all around

At a shotgun wedding, here in this town

And I'm the victim, and oh yeah

Of a shotgun wedding

'Cause your father got the gun

And there ain't no place to run

Shotgun wedding, and oh yeah

My, my, my, my, my, oh yeah, somebody please, somebody, oh help me now, oh yeah

Now I got to find a job, yes I have

For you, me, the baby makes three

Shotgun (shotgun)

Shotgun (shotgun)

Shotgun (shotgun)

Shotgun (shotgun)

Shotgun (shotgun)

Shotgun (shotgun)

Shotgun wedding, and oh yeah

Do you take this woman to be your lawful wedded wife?

Oh yeah, yeah, I look around

And all I could see

And all I could see

All I could see yeah

Was shotgun (shotgun)

Shotgun (shotgun)

Shotgun (shotgun)

Shotgun (shotgun)

Shotgun wedding (shotgun)

Shotgun

Somebody please come rescue me

And oh yeah

Lord, lord, lord, shotgun (shotgun)

Shotgun (shotgun)

Shotgun wedding (shotgun)," sang Rob Rule on lead vocals and lead guitar, Rick Prentiss on bass guitar and backing vocals, and Cyril Platt on backing vocals and drums.

The Rolling Stones came back on the stage and joined Swagger the rockers for a number, which excited the crowd who were watching this fantastic sight, immensely. And they roared their approval with cheers, yells and applause, and were screaming with joy.

The song the Rolling Stones and Swagger the rockers had chosen, was, "It's All Over Now", which was released on 2nd July 1964, on Decca records, that reached number one, and charted for a whopping, huge, 15 weeks.

"Well, baby used to stay out all night long

She made me cry, she done me wrong

She hurt me eyes open, that's no lie

Tables turn and now her turn to cry

Because I used to love her, but it's all over now

Because I used to love her, but it's all over now

Well, she used to run around with every man in town
Spent all my money, playing her high class game
She put me out, it was a pity how I cried
Tables turn and now her turn to cry
Because I used to love her, but it's all over now
Because I used to love her, but it's all over now
Musical break, guitar solo
Well, I used to wake in the morning, get my breakfast in bed
When I'd gotten worried, she'd ease my aching head
But now she's here and there with every man in town
Still trying to take me for that same old clown
Because I used to love her, but it's all over now
Because I used to love her, but it's all over now
Because I used to love her, but it's all over now," sang Mick Jagger and Rob Rule on lead vocals, with Rick Prentiss on bass guitar, along with Bill Wyman, also on bass guitar, Cyril Platt and Charlie Watts on drums, and Brian Jones on lead guitar and backing vocals. The sound was great and the crowd's appreciation was just as good. They cheered loudly.

The Small Faces returned on to the stage and replaced The Rolling Stones and Swagger the rockers, and they performed another one of their songs, "My Mind's Eye", which was released on Decca records on 7th November 1966, where it reached number 4, and charted for 11 weeks.

"I sit here every day, looking at the sky
Ever wondering why, I dream my dreams away
And I'm living for today, in my mind's eye
Things are clearer than before
Showing me the way, asking me to stay
I'll never close the door

To all these things and more
In my mind's eye
Everybody I know says I've changed, yeah
Laughing behind their hands
I think they're strange
People running everywhere
Running through my life
I couldn't give a care
Because they'll never see
All that I can see, with my mind's eye
La, la, la, la, la, la, la, la, la, la, la, la, la, la, la, la, la, la, la,
La, la, la, la, la, la, la,
In my mind's eye
Ah, ah, ah, ah, ah, ah, ah, ah, ah, ah, ah, ah, ah, ah, ah, ah, ah,
ah, ah, ah,
Ah, ah, ah, ah, ah, ah, ah,
In my mind's eye
Ah, ah, ah, ah, ah, ah, ah, ah, ah, ah, ah, ah, ah, ah, ah, ah, ah,
ah, ah, ah, ah,
Ah, ah, ah, ah, ah, ah, ah,
In my mind's eye," sang Steve Marriott on lead vocals and lead guitar, backed up superbly by Ronnie Lane on backing vocals and bass guitar, Kenney Jones on drums, and Ian McLagan on keyboards and backing vocals.
The crowd screamed with joy and elation at this brilliant performance by The Small Faces.
The Who then appeared on the stage and replaced The Small Faces, and the crowd went berserk at the sight of seeing one great group replacing another great group. The song they chose to sing was "Happy Jack", which was released on 15th December

1966, on Reaction Records, reaching number 3, and it stayed in the chart for 11 weeks.

"Happy Jack wasn't old

But he was a man

He lived in the sand

At the Isle of Man

The kids would all sing

He would take the wrong key

So they rode on his head in their furry donkey

The kids couldn't hurt Jack

They tried and tried and tried

They dropped things on his back

And lied and lied and lied and lied and lied

But they couldn't stop Jack or the waters lapping

And they couldn't prevent Jack from feeling happy

But they couldn't stop Jack or the waters lapping

And they couldn't prevent Jack from feeling happy

The kids couldn't hurt Jack

They tried and tried and tried

They dropped things on his back

And lied and lied and lied and lied and lied

But they couldn't stop Jack or the waters lapping

And they couldn't prevent Jack from feeling happy, I saw you!" sang Roger Daltrey on lead vocals, Pete Townshend on backing vocals and lead guitar, John Entwistle on bass guitar and Keith Moon on drums.

The crowd went wild. They screamed their appreciation. The show had concluded and everyone was happy. The gig had been a great success in Johannnesburg and everyone went home happy.

Chapter Nine

The mods and rockers roadshow continued across the globe, as Swagger the mods, Swagger the rockers, The Rolling Stones, The Kinks, The Small Faces and The Who were joined by Dave Dee, Dozy, Beaky, Mick and Tich and Manfred Mann, and they all jetted off to the United States of America for the next leg of their world tour, with California being the first destination in a series of gigs, starting on the west coast, and then visiting the USA as a whole, taking in many of the large cities of the country. The first stop was Disneyland, Anaheim, California. Everyone was excited. None of the guys in any of the bands had visited Disneyland or California before, so there was excitement in the air.

Anaheim was founded by fifty German families in 1857 and incorporated as the second city in Los Angeles County on 18th March 1876. Orange County was split off from Los Angeles County in 1889 and Anaheim remained largely an agricultural community until Disneyland opened in 1955. This led to the construction of several hotels and motels around the area and the residential districts in Anaheim. The city also developed into an industrial centre producing electronics, aircraft parts and canned fruit. Anaheim is a charter city, meaning the governing system is defined by the city's own charter document, rather than solely by general law. Anaheim means "home by the Santa Anna River" in German. To the Spanish speaking neighbours, the settlement was known as "Campo Aleman". The fifty families of settlers were mechanics, carpenters and craftsmen, with no experience in wine-making. And the community set aside 40 acres for a town centre and a school to be built. The first home was built in 1857. And a hotel in 1871. The Anaheim Gazette newspaper was established in 1810. The census of 1870 reported a population of 565 for the Anaheim district, and for 25 years, the area was the largest wine producers in California. In 1884, a disease infected the grapevines and by the following year, the entire industry was destroyed. Other crops, such as walnuts, lemons and oranges soon filled the void. Fruit and vegetables became viable cash crops, when the Los Angeles Orange County region was connected to the continental railroad network in 1887.

By the mid 1960's, the city's explosive growth would attract a Major League Baseball team, the California Angels, relocating from Los Angeles to Anaheim in 1966, where they have remained ever since. Construction of the Disneyland theme park began on 16th July 1954 and opened to the public on 17th July 1955. The location was formerly 160 acres of orange and walnut trees.

World Cup 1966 fever was upon England. The big tournament had arrived at last. Everyone had been waiting patiently for the showpiece of international football to begin, and now it was ready to explode in front of everyones eyes. On television, radio, cinemas all around the world, and football grounds scattered all around England. Excitement had been bubbling for weeks, as the fever came to the boil, and England played their first World Cup match against Uruguay at Wembley stadium on Monday 11th July 1966, at 7 30 pm, with 87, 148 people in attendance.

England's team was as follows, and Uruguay's team was as follows,

1, Gordon Banks, Leicester City   1, Ladislao Mazurkiewicz, Penarol

| 2, George Cohen, Fulham | 2, Horacio Troche, |
| captain, Cerro | |

2, George Cohen, Fulham   2, Horacio Troche,
captain, Cerro

3, Ray Wilson, Everton   3, Jorge
Manicera, Nacional

4, Nobby Stiles, Manchester Uniited   15, Luis Ubina,
Rampla Juniors

5, Jack Charlton, Leeds United   5, Nestor
Goncalves, Penarol

6, Bobby Moore, captain, West Ham United   6, Omar Caetano,
Penarol

7, Alan Ball, Blackpool   7, Julio Cesar
Cortes, Penarol

8, Jimmy Greaves, Tottenham Hotspur   18, Milton Viera,
Nacional

9, Bobby Charlton, Manchester United   19, Hector Silva,
Penarol

21, Roger Hunt, Liverpool   10, Pedro Rocha,
Penarol

11, John Connelly, Manchester United   11, Domingo
Perez, Nacional

Istvan Zsolt of Hungary was the referee.

England were held 0-0 by the rugged South Americans, although Bobby Charlton almost broke the deadlock with a screamer. John Connelly missed two late chances and Jimmy Greaves was stifled by the oppressive marking. It appeared that the South Americans had come for a draw, and they celebrated at the end of the match as if they had won. They had played with nine men in defence. The crowd in the stadium and the millions of viewers all around the world were not impressed with this opening game, and the crowd at Wembley turned on the dour visiting team from Uruguay, with jeers and boos at the final whistle.

Before the game began, the Queen had opened the tournament, in a bright, colourful spectacle. However, England started with a point in the bank, a clean sheet, their third successive shut out, but had failed to score for the first time in 12 matches. But it didn't matter. They had continued with their unbeaten run, through 1966, after their seven successive victories in the friendlies, leading up to the World Cup tournament. And Alf Ramsey, who was confident of England winning the World Cup would be looking for an improvement in front of the goal in their next match, and hoped they would score a hatful and win against Mexico on Saturday 16th July 1966.

As England drew their opening World Cup match, Swagger the mods, Swagger the rockers and The Rolling Stones,The Kinks, The Who, The Small Faces, Dave Dee, Dozy, Beaky, Mick and Tich and Manfred Mann were preparing for their show at Disneyland in California, thousands of miles away.

It was Dave Dee, Dozy, Beaky, Mick and Tich that opened the show, along with the six go-go dancers, Jilly Jacobs, Jackie Jones, Rosie Wright, Becky Bright, Erica Shaw and Lily Lewis, looking hot and sultry in yellow bikinis.

The opening song was "Bend It", which was released on 15th September 1966, on Fontana records, where it spent 12 weeks in the chart, and reached number 2.

"Bend it, bend it, just a little bit
And take it easy, show you're likin' it
And lover, you know that we're gonna hit
The heights 'cause I'm sure that we're made to fit
Together just like pieces of a

Jigsaw puzzle, what's the hustle
Bend it, bend it, just a little more
Without you baby, I'm so insecure
But you can make me feel that I am sure
I've got a sickness only you can cure
So just relax, there's stacks of time, but honey
Please don't tease me, try to please me
Oh yeah, that's good, oh yes, ah yes
Bend it, bend it, just a little bit
And take it easy, show you're likin' it
And lover, you know that we're gonna hit
The heights, 'cause I'm sure that we're made to fit
Together just like pieces of a
Jigsaw puzzle, what's the hustle
Bend it, bend it, just a little bit
And take it easy, show you're likin' it
And ahhh, show me now, yeah, that's right
Ah, oh yeah, yeah that's right
C'mon now, right, right, right

Right, right, right, right, right, right, right, right," sang Dave Dee (Dave Harmon) on lead vocals, Dozy (Trevor Ward-Davies) on bass guitar, Beaky (John Dymond) on rhythm guitar, Mick (Michael Wilson) on drums and Tich (Ian Amey) on lead guitar and electric mandolin, with all the group members assisting in backing vocals.

The go-go dancers moved beautifully to the music played by Dave Dee, Dozy, Beaky, Mick and Tich, and the crowd appreciated both the band and the dancers, for their fantastic performance. The group stayed on the stage to do another song, "Hideaway". A track that was released on 9th June 1966 on

Fontana records, which reached number 10, charted for 11 weeks and was popular with the California audience.

"Hideaway (come on)
Far from the light of day (come on)
Leaving the world behind
And out of mind
A place we'll find
Where we can hideaway
Hideaway (come on)
Where we can go and play (come on)
Just like the kids in school
We'll act the fool
Break every rule
In our own hideaway
Come on baby, they'll never find us here
Made sure the coast was clear
There's not a thing left to fear
Hideaway (come on)
That's where we're gonna stay (come on)
In just a little time
You'll feel so fine
I'll make you mine
In our own hideaway
Guitar solo
Hideaway (come on)
Far from the light of day (come on)
Leaving the world behind
And out of mind
A place we'll find

Where we can hideaway," sang Dave Dee on lead vocals, Dozy on backing vocals and bass guitar, Beaky on rhythm guitar, Mick on drums and backing vocals and Tich on lead guitar and backing vocals.

The crowd were super excited and showed great passion in their applause and cheering.

The third song was "Hold Tight", a favourite with the Californian crowd. It brought the house down.

"Hold tight, count to three
Gotta stay close by me
And hold tight sing and shout
Just ride my round-about
And hold tight, shut your eyes
Girl you suit me for size
Forget the other guys
You'll never fall, each time you call
Hold tight, hold tight, hold tight
Hold tight, make me feel
What you say is for real
And hold tight carousel
Girl you'll soon ring my bell
And hold tight we will fly
Swingin' low swingin' high
We're gonna make the sky
You'll never fall, each time you call
Hold tight, hold tight, hold tight
Guitar solo
Hold tight, count to three
Gotta stay close by me
And hold tight, sing and shout

Just ride my round-about
And hold tight shut your eyes
Girl you suit me for size
Forget the other guys
You'll never fall, each time you call
Hold tight, hold tight, hold tight," sang and played Dave Dee,
Dozy, Beaky, Mick and Tich.

Chapter Ten

Dave Dee, Dozy, Beaky, Mick and Tich left the stage to a
resounding round of applause, with hearty cheers and screaming
of adulation from the Disneyland crowd. The atmosphere was
fantastic.

The rides were still taking place in and around the vast area of
the amusements park, as the pop concert was taking place, and
there was the smell of food, burgers, onions, french fries, fish
and chips, doughnuts, and a whiff of diesel from the power
generators.

It all added up into a crescendo of bubbling excitement, as the
show continued, with Manfred Mann taking to the stage for
their turn in front of the massive audience, which must have
reached over one hundred thousand fans. There were rows of
people that seemed to go on forever.

They began with "Just Like A Woman", a Bob Dylan song, which
Manfred Mann covered and released as a single on 4th August
1966 on Fontana records, where it reached number 10 and
charted for 10 weeks.

The crowd cheered with approval, as the song began.

"She takes just like a woman, yes she does
And she makes love just like a woman, yes she does
And she aches just like a woman
But she breaks just like a little girl
Nobody feels any pain
Tonight as I stand inside the rain
Everybody knows that baby's got new clothes
But lately I see her ribbons and her bows
Have fallen from her curls
She takes just like a woman, yes she does
And she makes love just like a woman, yes she does
And she aches just like a woman
But she breaks just like a little girl
Queen Mary, she's my friend
Yes I believe I'll go and see her again
Nobody has to guess that baby can't be blessed
Till she finally sees that she's like all the rest
With her fog, her amphetamine and her pearls
She takes just like a woman, yes she does
And she makes love just like a woman, yes she does
And she aches just like a woman
But she breaks just like a little girl
It was raining from the first
And I was dying there of thirst, so I came in here
When your long time curse hurts
But what's worse is this pain in here
I can't stay in here, ain't it clear that
I just can't fit?
Yes I believe it's time for us to quit
When we meet again introduced as friends

Please don't let on that you knew me when

I was hungry and it was your world

Ah, you fake just like a woman, yes you do

And you make love just like a woman, yes you do

Then you ache just like a woman

But you break just like a little girl," sang Mike d'Abo on lead vocals, singing the full Bob Dylan version as a treat to the Californian crowd of fans, who adored both the Manfred Mann cover and the Bob Dylan original.

Paul Jones and Mike d'Abo were present on the tour, as Paul Jones was on the verge of leaving the band to go solo, and Mike d'Abo was on the verge of joining the group as Paul Jones replacement. So they sang their own songs individually.

With Mike d'Abo, the lead vocalist on "Just Like A Woman", was Manfred Mann on keyboards, Mike Hugg on drums, Tom McGuinness on lead guitar and Jack Bruce on bass guitar, with all the musicians contributing to the backing vocals throughout the track.

The next song Manfred Mann performed as a group was "5,4,3,2,1" that was released on 23rd January 1964 on the HMV POP record label, which reached number 5 in the chart, and spent 13 weeks there. Paul Jones entered the stage to take over from Mike d'Abo, as the lead vocalist, and was equipped with a harmonica that opened the song.

"(Five, four, three, two, one) slowly

(Five, four, three, two, one)

(Five, four, three, two, one)

(Five, four, three, two, one)

(Five, four, three, two, one)

(Five, four, three, two, one)

(Five, four, three, two, one)

Onwards onwards rode the six hundred

(Five, four, three, two, one)

Down the valley on their horses they thundered

(Five, four, three, two, one)

Ah, but was it them who really blundered

(Five, four, three, two, one)

(Uh huh, it was the Manfreds)

(Five, four, three, two, one)

(Five, four, three, two, one)

The Trojans waited at the gate for weeks

(Five, four, three, two, one)

In a wooden horse to the city they sneaked

(Five, four, three, two, one)

Who let them in, was it the Greeks?

(Five, four, three, two, one)

(Uh huh, it was the Manfreds)

(Five, four, three, two, one)

(Five, four, three, two, one)

(Five, four, three, two, one)

(Five, four, three, two, one)

(Five, four, three, two, one)

(Uh huh, it was the Manfreds)

(Five, four, three, two, one) slowly," sang Paul Jones on lead vocals and harmonica, Manfred Mann on keyboards and backing vocals, Mike Hugg on drums and backing vocals, Tom McGuinness on lead guitar and backing vocals, and Jack Bruce on bass guitar and backing vocals, with the track written by Mike Hugg, Paul Jones and Manfred Mann.

The crowd went wild, cheered, clapped, screamed and whistled in appreciation.

The band swiftly moved onto their next song, "If You Gotta Go, Go Now", another Bob Dylan track, that was released on 16th September 1965 on the HMV POP record label, which reached number 2, and spent 12 weeks on the chart.

Jilly, Jackie, Rosie, Becky, Erica and Lily, the go-go dancers had moved beautifully to the previous song, with elegant grace, panache and verve, and they were dressed in fetching, matching, black bikinis, as it was extremely hot and humid in California, and they continued to gyrate, hustle, shuffle and grind to this next track, with artistic flair.

"Listen to me baby

I'm tryin' to make you see

That I want to be with you, girl

If you want to be with me

But if you gotta go

Well, that's alright

But if you gotta go, go now

Or else you gotta stay all night

I am just a poor boy, baby

Tryin' to connect

But I don't want you thinkin'

Oh, that I ain't got any respect

But if you gotta go

Well, it's alright

But if you gotta go, go now

Or else you gotta stay all night

Now I'm not trying to question you

To take part in any quiz

It's just that I don't have a watch
And you keep askin' me what time it is
But if you gotta go
Well, it's alright
But if you gotta go, go now
Or else you gotta stay all night
Now I don't want to make you give anything
You never gave before
It's just that I'll be sleepin' soon
It'll be too dark for you to find the door
But if you gotta go
Well, it's alright
But if you gotta go, go now
Or else you gotta stay all night," sang Paul Jones on lead vocals and harmonica, Manfred Mann on keyboards, Mike Hugg on drums, Tom McGuinness on lead guitar and Jack Bruce on bass guitar, and all assisting with the backing vocals.

The crowd lifted the roof off the building, cheering passionately, ardently and excitedly, as the band finished their spell on the stage, with a fabulous performance.

Swagger the mods took their place on the stage, and the crowd cheered and screamed loudly. They had heard a lot about these guys and were excited to see them in the flesh. The girls in particular were very excited and impressed. They whistled and howled.

The go-go dancers were off the stage to change into matching red bikinis, and as soon as they returned, Swagger the mods started their song, a cover version of "Reach Out I'll Be There", originally recorded by The Four Tops on the Tamla Motown record label, that reached number one, was released on 13th October 1966, and charted for 16 weeks.

"Yah, now if you feel that you (can't go on)
Because (all of your hope is gone)
And your life is filled with (much confusion)
Until happiness is (just an illusion)
And your world around is crumblin' down
Darling (reach out) come on girl, (reach out) for me
(Reach out) (reach out, for me)
Hah, I'll be there, with a love that will shelter you
I'll be there with a love that will see you through
When you feel lost and about (to give up)
'Cause your best is (just ain't good enough)
And you feel the world has (grown cold)
And you're (drifting out all on your own)
And you (need a hand to hold)
Darlin' (reach out) come on girl, reach out for me
(Reach out) reach out for me
Hah, I'll be there to love and comfort you
And I'll be there to cherish and care for you
(I'll be there to always see you through)
(I'll be there to love and comfort you)
I can tell by the way you (hang your head)
You're without love and now (you're afraid)
And through your tears you (look around)
But there's (no peace of mind to be found)
I know what you're thinkin'
You're alone now, no love of your own
But darlin' (reach out) come on girl, reach out for me
(Reach out) reach out

Just look over your shoulder
I'll be there to give you all the love you need
And I'll be there, you can always depend on me
I'll be there, to give you all the love you need
I'll be there, you can always depend on me
I'll be there," sang Ted on lead vocals and lead guitar, Sid on backing vocals and drums, and Fred on bass guitar and additional backing vocals.

Swagger the mods left the stage and were replaced swiftly by Swagger the rockers, and they received warm applause and constant cheering.

They moved straight into their number "I Got You", recorded by James Brown, which Swagger the rockers covered exceptionally well. This track was released by James Brown on 24th February 1966 on the Pye International record label, where it reached number 29, and charted for 6 weeks.

"Whoa! I feel good, I knew that I would, now
I feel good, I knew that I would, now
So good, so good, I got you
Whoa! I feel nice, like sugar and spice
I feel nice, like sugar and spice
So nice, so nice, I got you
When I hold you in my arms
I know that I can't do no wrong
And when I hold you in my arms
My love won't do you no harm
And I feel nice, like sugar and spice
I feel nice, like sugar and spice
So nice, so nice, I got you
When I hold you in my arms

I know that I can't do no wrong
And when I hold you in my arms
My love can't do me no harm
And I feel nice, like sugar and spice
I feel nice, like sugar and spice
So nice, so nice, 'cause I got you
Whoa! And I feel good, I knew that I would, now
I feel good, I knew that I would
So good, so good, 'cause I got you
So good, so good, 'cause I got you
So good, so good, 'cause I got you
Hey

Oh-whoo," sang Rob Rule on lead vocals and lead guitar, Rick Prentiss on saxophone and backing vocals, with Cyril Platt on drums and backing vocals.

The crowd cheered relentlessly and applauded with enthusiasm, as they fully demonstrated their appreciation. The lads in Swagger the rockers also appreciated the applause and adulation and moved onto another number, joined by Swagger the mods, for a collaboration on "Um,Um,Um", originally recorded by Major Lance. This track was released on 13th February 1964 on the Columbia record label. It reached number 40 in the chart and spent 2 weeks there, and was written by Curtis Mayfield.

Chapter Eleven

"Walking through the park, it wasn't quite dark
There was a man sitting on a bench
Out of the crowd as his head lowly bowed

He just moaned and he made no sense
He'd just go
Um, um, um, um, um
Um, um, um, um, um, um
Um, um, um, um, um
Um, um, um, um, um, um
I just couldn't help myself
Yes, I was born, with a curious mind
I asked this man just what did he mean
When he moaned, if he'd be so kind
And he'd just go
Um, um, um, um, um
Um, um, um, um, um, um
Um, um, um, um, um
Um, um, um, um, um, um
Now that I've grown up
And the woman I love, she has gone
Now that I'm a man, I think I understand
Sometimes everyone must sing this song
Listen to me sing
Um, um, um, um, um
Um, um, um, um, um, um
Um, um, um, um, um
Um, um, um, um, um, um
Can't you hear me now
Um, um, um, um, um
Um, um, um, um, um, um
Um, um, um, um, um
Um, um, um, um, um, um
Everybody now

Um, um, um, um, um

Um, um, um, um, um, um

Um, um, um, um, um

Um, um, um, um, um, um

One more time, now

Um, um, um, um, um

Um, um, um, um, um, um

Um, um, um, um, um

Um, um, um, um, um, um," sang Ted Rummy and Rob Rule on lead vocals and lead guitars, assisted by Sid Cross and Cyril Platt on drums and backing vocals and Fred Bloggs and Rick Prentiss on bass guitars.

The crowd went crazy in California and gave the two bands a standing ovation.

Then there was a surprise, as Swagger the mods and Swagger the rockers moved aside and brought the six go-go dancers from the front of the stage to the microphones, to perform a song. This was the first time that Jilly, Jackie, Rosie, Becky, Erica and Lily had sang in public. And they were as excited as the crowd. There was an enormous cheer, lots of wolf-whistles, applause and screaming, as the music began. It was "Rescue Me", a song originally recorded by Fontella Bass, that the go-go dancers were going to perform. This track was released on 2nd December 1965, on the Chess record label, which reached number 11 and charted for 10 weeks.

"Rescue me

Take me in your arms

Rescue me

I want your tender charm

'Cause I'm lonely

And I'm blue
I need you
And your love too
Come on and rescue me
Come on baby and rescue me
Come on baby and rescue me
'Cause I need you by my side
Can't you see that I'm lonely
Rescue me
Come on and take my heart
Take your love and conquer every part
'Cause I'm lonely
And I'm blue
I need you
And your love too
Come on and rescue me
Come on, baby, and rescue me
Come on, baby, and rescue me
'Cause I need you by my side
Can't you see that I'm lonely
Rescue me
Take me in your arms
Rescue me
I want your tender charm
'Cause I'm lonely
And I'm blue
I need you
And your love too
Come on and rescue me (come on baby)
Take me baby (take me baby)

Hold me baby (hold me baby)
Love me baby (love me baby)
Can't you see that I need you baby
Can't you see that I'm lonely
Rescue me
Come on and take my hand
C'mon baby and be my man
'Cause I love you
'Cause I want you
Can't you see that I'm lonely
Mmm-hmm (mmm-hmm)
Mmm-hmm (mmm-hmm)
Take me baby (take me baby)
Love me baby (love me baby)
Need me baby (need me baby)
Mmm-hmm (mmm-hmm)
Mmm can't you see that I'm lonely
Rescue me
Rescue me
Mmm-hmm, mmm-hmm," sang Jilly Jacobs on lead vocals, ably assisted by Jackie Jones, Rosie Wright, Becky Bright, Erica Shaw and Lily Lewis, on backing vocals.

The crowd erupted with elation, joy and delight at this fantastic performance, and the go-go dancers continued with another song, "Heaven Must Have Sent You", a track by the Elgins, that was released on 1st May 1971, in the United Kingdom, which charted for 13 weeks, and was released on the Tamla Motown record label, and made number 3 in the top 20. The go-go dancers had picked up on the song that had circulated around the United Kingdom before the official release there, and it was popular in 1966 in the United States of America.

"I've cried through many endless nights
Just holding my pillow tight
Then you came into my lonely days
With your tender love and your sweet ways
Now I don't know where you come from baby
Don't know where you've been, my baby
Heaven must have sent you
Into my arms
Now in the mornin' when I awake
There's a smile upon my face
You've touched my heart with gladness
Wiped away all my sadness
So long I've needed love right near me
A soft voice to cheer me
Heaven must have sent you, honey
Into my life, ooh
It's heaven in your arms
It's the sweetness of your charms
Makes me love you more each day
In your arms I wanna stay
Wanna thank you for the joy you brought me
Thank you for the things you taught me
Thank you for holding me close
When I needed you the most
Now, I don't know much about you, baby
But I know I can't live without you
Heaven must have sent you
To love only me, ooh

It's heaven in your arms
Boy, it's the sweetness of your charms
Makes me love you more each day
In your arms I wanna stay
It's heaven in your arms
It's the sweetness of your charms
It makes me love you more each day
In your arms I wanna stay
It's heaven in your arms
Boy, it's the sweetness of your charms
Makes me love you more each day
In your arms I wanna stay," sang Jilly, Jackie, Rosie, Becky, Erica and Lily, each taking the lead vocals, in a polished, professional, epic cover version of the classic song.

The crowd erupted into fits of excitement, as the go-go dancers left the stage, and the reception was terrific, with loud whistles, applause and appreciation. The noise didn't die down. The crowd wanted more from the go-go dancers, and they weren't disappointed, as the six go-go dancers came back for an encore.

They sang "Where Did Our Love Go", a track originally recorded by The Supremes, which the go-go dancers loved, and this song was recorded on 3rd September 1964, on the Stateside record label, and reached number 3, charting for 14 weeks.

"Baby baby, baby don't leave me
Ooh, please don't leave me, all by myself
I've got this burning, burning, yearning, feelin' inside me
Ooh, deep inside me, and it hurts so bad
You came into my heart (baby baby) so tenderly (where did our love go)

With a burning love (baby baby)
That stings like a bee (baby baby) (ooh baby baby)
Now that I surrender (baby baby)
So helplessly (where did our love go)
You now want to leave (baby baby)
Ooh, you wanna leave me (baby baby)
Ooh (baby baby)
(Baby baby) (Where did our love go?)
Ooh don't you want me? (baby baby)
Don't you want me no more? (baby baby)
(Ooh baby)
Saxophone solo
Baby, baby (where did our love go?) (baby baby)
And all your promises, of a love forevermore! (baby baby)
(baby baby)
I've got this burning, burning, yearning, feelin' inside me (baby
baby)
(Where did our love go)
Ooh deep inside me, and it hurts so bad (baby baby) (baby
baby)
(Ooh baby baby)
Before you won my heart (baby baby)
You were a perfect guy (baby baby) (where did our love go)
But now that you got me
You wanna leave me behind (baby baby) (baby baby) (where did
our love go)
Ooh baby
Baby, baby, baby don't leave me
Ooh, please don't leave me, all by myself (baby baby)
Ooh baby (baby baby)

Don't you want me (baby baby)

Don't you want me no more? (oh baby)" sang Jilly Jacobs, Jackie Jones, Rosie Wright, Becky Bright, Erica Shaw and Lily Lewis.

The crowd went crazy for this song, and cheered relentlessly. It was fabulous by the go-go dancers. They really had done a first class cover version, smashing it out of the park. They were thrilled. The crowd were thrilled. Everyone backstage were thrilled. The go-go dancers had arrived on the music scene.

The go-go dancers made their way quickly to the front of the stage to dance again, and were replaced at the microphones by Booker T and the MG's, who received a huge reception of cheers, howls, and screaming, and they went straight into their first number, "Red Beans and Rice" an instrumental, which didn't chart in Great Britain, but was a massive hit in the clubs, bars, dance halls and at parties, throughout the United Kingdom, Europe and the United States of America. It was released on 17th November 1965, on the Stax record label. It was the B side to "Be My Lady", with both tracks having great success on the dance floor. It went down well today, in a groovy way. The band played another instrumental, "Green Onions", from the album of the same name. It was released by Booker T and the MG's on 25th July 1964, and made number 11 in the album chart, spending four weeks there, and was released on the London record label.

The go-go dancers, Jilly, Jackie, Rosie, Becky, Erica and Lily led the dancing, by grinding, hustling, doing the pony, and throughly cavorting in a sensual, sexy manner, thrusting their hips wildly. Everyone enjoyed both the music and the dancers.

Booker T and the MG's played "Rinky Dink", from the "Green Onions" album and also "I Got A Woman", "Mo Onions", "Twist and Shout", "Behave Yourself", "Stranger On The Shore" and "Lonely Avenue", from the same album, with the instrumentals mixing and blending into one another with precision and aplomb.

The go-go dancers excelled and were really funking it up, with skill, panache and passion, as they threw shapes in all directions. This was a fantastic display of go-go dancing, as the women displayed finesse and style.

Booker T and the MG's finished their set with the track "Time is Tight", which reached number 4 in the singles chart and spent 18 whopping weeks there. It was released on Stax records on 7th May 1969.

The California concert was now over. The guys in the bands were ready to jet off to Florida for the next leg of this awesome world tour of mods and rockers.

Chapter Twelve

Over to Wembley Stadium, in England, for the 1966 World Cup tournament. The games resumed, the action returned and the results of the first round of the competition were in, and were as follows;

Group 1

England 0 Uruguay 0

France 1 Mexico 1

Group 2

West Germany 5 Switzerland 0

Argentina 2 Spain 1

Group 3

Brazil 2 Bulgaria 0

Portugal 3 Hungary 1

Group 4

USSR 3 North Korea 0

Italy 2 Chile 0

England's next match was on Saturday 16th July, 1966, with a kick off time of 7 30 pm, at Wembley Stadium, where the attendance was a very healthy 92,570, and the referee was Concetto Lo Bello from Syracuse, in Italy.

England lined up as follows for the match against Mexico, in round 2 of the group games.

1, Gordon Banks, Leicester City, aged 28, 29 caps, goalkeeper

2, George Cohen, Fulham, aged 26, 26 caps, right full back

3, Ray Wilson, Everton, aged 31, 47 caps, left full back

4, Nobby Stiles, Manchester United, aged 24, 16 caps, midfield

5, Jack Charlton, Leeds United, aged 31, 18 caps, central defender

6, Bobby Moore, West Ham United, captain, aged 25, 43 caps, central defender

16, Martin Peters, West Ham United, aged 22, 19 caps, midfield

8, Jimmy Greaves, Tottenham Hotspur, aged 26, 53 caps, forward

9, Bobby Charlton, Manchester United, aged 28, 70 caps, midfield

21, Roger Hunt, Liverpool, aged 27, 15 caps, forward

19, Terry Paine, Southampton, aged 27, 4 caps, midfield

The England manager was Alf Ramsey aged 46.

The Mexico team lined up as follows;

12, Ignacio Calderon, Club Deportivo Guadalajara, aged 22, goalkeeper

2, Arturo Chaires, Club Deportivo Guadalajara, aged 29, defender

4, Jose de Jesus del Muro Lopez, Veracruz, aged 29, defender

5, Ignacio Jauregui, Club de Football Monterrey, aged 27, defender

14, Gabriel Nunez, Zacatepec, aged 24, defender

3, Gustavo Pena, Oro Guadalajara, captain, aged 24, defender

15, Guillermo Hernandez, Atlas Guadalajara, aged 24, midfield

20, Enrique Borja, Pumas, aged 20, forward

6, Isidoro Diaz, Club Deportivo Guadalajara, aged 26, midfield

8, Aaron Padilla Gutierrez, Pumas, aged 24, forward

19, Salavdor Reyes Monteon, Club Deportivo Guadalajara, aged 29, forward

The manager was Ignacio Trelles, aged 49. The linesmen were Menachem Ashkenazi of Israel and Duk-Ryung Choi of North Korea.

After 37 minutes, Bobby Charlton scored an absolutely stunning goal, to get England on the way, with a shot from 25 yards, after he ran with the ball from the halfway line, jinking, shuffling, dodging and weaving with great balance, skill and technique. He hit the ball so hard it flew into the back of the net like a rocket, and had to be one of the best ever goals seen at Wembley Stadium. It lifted the team to glory, and Roger Hunt was on hand to tap in a second goal in the 75th minute, to settle the English nerves, and give the Three Lions a 2-0 win.

The game was frantic, with both sides creating chances, but it was Bobby Charlton that stole the show, and showed the world how great he is in front of the goal. The shot was hit with so much venom and power, it almost broke the net. The crowd went wild with delight and it got England their first win of the tournament, which was also their 12th consecutive match without defeat.

The second round of group games had taken place, and the results of these matches were as follows;

Group One

England 2 Mexico 0

Uruguay 2 France 1

Group Two

Spain 2 Switzerland 1

West Germany 0 Argentina 0

Group Three

Hungary 3 Brazil 1

Portugal 3 Bulgaria 0

Group Four

North Korea 1 Chile 1

USSR 1 Italy 0

The next match for England was against France on Wednesday 20th July 1966, at 7 30 pm, in the final group game of the tournament, and England lined up as follows;

1, Gordon Banks, Leicester City, aged 28, goalkeeper

2, George Cohen, Fulham, aged 26, right full back

3, Ray Wilson, Everton, aged 31, left full back

4, Nobby Stiles, Manchester United, aged 24, midfield

5, Jack Charlton, Leeds United, aged 31, central defender

6, Bobby Moore, West Ham United, captain, aged 25, central defender

20, Ian Callaghan, Liverpool, aged 24, midfield

8, Jimmy Greaves, Tottenham Hotspur, aged 26, forward

9, Bobby Charlton, Manchester United, aged 28, attacking midfield

21, Roger Hunt, Liverpool, aged 27, forward

16, Martin Peters, West Ham United, aged 22, midfield

The referee was Aturo Yamasaki, aged 37, a Peruvian Mexican, born in Lima, Peru, in 1929, and the attendance was 98, 270.

France lined up like this.

1, Marcel Aubour, goalkeeper, OGC Nice, aged 26

2, Marcel Artelesa, midfield, Olympique Marseille, aged 28

5, Bernard Bosquier, defender, AS Saint-Etienne, aged 24

6, Robert Budzynski, defender, FC Nantes, aged 26

12, Jean Djorkaeff, defender, Olympique Marseille, aged 26

16, Robert Herbin, midfield, AS Saint-Etienne, aged 27

4, Joseph Bonnel, midfield, US Valenciennes-Anzin, aged 27

15, Yves Herbet, midfield, CS Sedan, aged 20

20, Jacques "Jacky" Simon, forward, FC Nantes, aged 25

13, Phillipe Gondet, forward, FC Nantes, aged 24

14, Gerard Hausser, forward, RC Strasbourg, aged 24

The manager was Henri Guerin, born on August 27 1921, aged 44.

England knocked France out of the World Cup with two goals from Roger Hunt. The first was in the 38th minute, after a cross by Jimmy Greaves was headed against the post by Jack Charlton, and Hunt was there to tap the ball into the empty net. Then Hunt scored his, and England's second, after 75 minutes, with a powerful header, that had too much pace and strength for Aubour, in goal, for the French. Hunt brilliantly hung high in the air, and powered the ball into the back of the net, with a great headed finish.

Nobby Stiles was booked, but was lucky to stay on the pitch, as he was involved in many incidents. In the 55th minute, he threw a punch at Robert Herbin, but was not cautioned for that, although he received a harsh telling off from the referee. Later in the game, in the 74th minute, Stiles arm was raised to Bernard Bosquier, when he chased down a through ball, and he received a booking this time. Then Stiles clattered Jacques "Jacky" Simon from behind in the 75th minute, leaving the Frenchman injured, whilst England scored a goal, and Simon was carried off, and treated on the sidelines, but Stiles escaped a second booking and a sending off.

England had two goals disallowed. Firstly Jimmy Greaves was adjudged to be offside, when he met a Martin Peters headed knock-down from a Ian Callaghan cross on the right, in the 29th minute. And then, Bobby Charlton was adjudged to be offside in the 66th minute, despite being two yards onside, and behind the ball.

Jimmy Greaves needed 14 stitches to close a deep gash in his shin, after Joseph Bonnel raked his studs down his leg, and it changed Greaves life dramatically, as it put him out of the rest of this match. But would it end the star forward's World Cup campaign? The injury was so severe, Alf Ramsey needed to replace Greaves for the next match, in an effort to build upon the unbeaten start to the campaign.

England were now through to the knock-out stages, without their top striker, Greaves, and Geoff Hurst was called up to replace the injured star forward. Would Hurst take his big chance and make it impossible for Greaves to regain his place? The onus was on Hurst to impress.

England's next match was the quarter final game against Argentina on Saturday 23rd July 1966, at Wembley Stadium. The excitement was bubbling. England had done well in the group stages, winning two and drawing one, and they built up a crescendo of noise, fever and anticipation among the nation, from coast to coast and town to town, in the villages and cities, for a possible World Cup winning opportunity. How would Geoff Hurst cope with the pressure?

The round 3 group matches results were as follows;

Group One

Uruguay 0 Mexico 0

England 2 France 0

Group One table

1, England, played 3, won 2, drew 1, lost 0, goals for, 4, goals against, 0, +4, 5 points

2, Uruguay, played 3, won 1, drew 2, lost 0, goals for, 2, goals against, 1, +1, 4 points

3, Mexico, played 3, won 0, drew 2, lost 1, goals for, 1, goals against, 3, -2, 2 points

4, France, played 3, won 0, drew 1, lost 2, goals for, 2, goals against, 5, -3, 1 point

Group Two

Argentina 2 Switzerland 0

West Germany 2 Spain 1

Group Two table

1, West Germany, played 3, won 2, drew 1, lost 0, goals for, 7, goals against, 1, +6, 5 points

2, Argentina, played 3, won 2, drew 1, lost 0, goals for, 4, goals against, 1, +3, 5 points

3, Spain, played 3, won 1, drew 0, lost 2, goals for, 4, goals against, 5, -1, 2 points

4, Switzerland, played 3, won 0, drew 0, lost 3, 0 points, goals for, 1, goals against, 9, -8, 0 points

Group Three

Portugal 3 Brazil 1

Hungary 3 Bulgaria 1

Group Three table

1, Portugal, played 3, won 3, drew 0, lost 0, goals for, 9, goals against, 2, +7, 6 points

2, Hungary, played 3, won 2, drew 0, lost 1, goals for, 7, goals against, 5, +2, 4 points

3, Brazil, played 3, won 1, drew 0, lost 2, goals for, 4, goals against, 6, -2, 2 points

4, Bulgaria, played 3, won 0, drew 0, lost 3, goals for 1, goals against 8, -7, 0 points

Group Four

North Korea 1 Italy 0

USSR 2 Chile 1

Group Four table

1, USSR, played 3, won 3, drew 0, lost 0, goals for, 6, goals against, 1, +5, 6 points

2, North Korea, played 3, won 1, drew 1, lost 1, goals for, 2, goals against, 4, -2, 3 points

3, Italy, played 3, won 1, drew 0, lost 2, goals for, 2, goals against, 2, 0, 2 points

4, Chile, played 3, won 0, drew 1, lost 2, goals for, 2, goals against, 5, -3, 1 point

The quarter final matches were as follows;

England v Argentina

West Germany v Uruguay

Portugal v North Korea

USSR v Hungary.

England lined up against Argentina with this team;

1, Gordon Banks, Leicester City

2, George Cohen, Fulham

3, Ray Wilson, Everton

4, Nobby Stiles, Manchester United

5, Jack Charlton, Leeds United

6, Bobby Moore, captain, West Ham United

7, Alan Ball, Blackpool

16, Martin Peters, West Ham United

9, Bobby Charlton, Manchester United

10, Geoff Hurst, West Ham United

21, Roger Hunt, Liverpool

The match was played on Saturday 23rd July 1966, with a 3pm kick off. It was a game described by the Argentinians as "The Robbery Of The Century" or in Spanish, "El Robo Del Siglo".

Argentina lined up as follows;

1, Antonio Roma, goalkeeper, Boca Juniors, aged 34

8, Roberto Ferreiro, right full back, Independiente, aged 31

7, Silvio Marzolini, left full back, Boca Juniors, aged 25

4, Roberto Perfumo, central defender, Racing Club, aged 23

12, Rafael Albrecht, central defender, San Lorenzo, aged 24

10, Antonio Rattin, captain, midfield, Boca Juniors, aged 29

15, Jorge Solari, midfield, River Plate, aged 24

16, Alberto Mario Gonzalez, forward, Boca Juniors, aged 24

20, Ermindo Onega, attacking midfield, River Plate, aged 26

19, Luis Artime, striker, River Plate, aged 27

21, Oscar Mas, forward, River Plate, aged 19

The manager was Juan Carlos Lorenzo, and the referee was Rudolf Kreitlein from West Germany. The linesmen were Gottfried Dienst from Switzerland and Istvan Zsolt from Hungary.

What a match this was. With Geoff Hurst coming in as Jimmy Greaves replacement, and scoring the winner, with a sublime header of brilliance in the execution, as he directed the ball, by slicing it with his head majestically, into the back of the net, with panache, style and aplomb, which Bobby Charlton claimed was the best goal he had ever seen. It was enough for England to wrap up the game in their favour, and take them to the semi final of the World Cup. But the game was not without incident. Argentina had five players booked, including their captain Antonio Rattin, who was booked twice and sent off. But he refused to go, and was visible on the pitch for 8 minutes. When he eventually went off, he was escorted by two policemen, and twisted the pendant of the corner flag that displayed the England emblem of Three Lions and the St George's Cross. He also decided to make his way to the red carpet and sat down on the area that is designated for the Queen of England only. She was not present at the match, but it was regarded as an insult to the English.

And England out-scored Argentina 30-8 for fouls committed, which was nearly three times as many, but they didn't have a single player booked. Although the Charlton brothers, Bobby and Jack both received a ticking-off from the referee, it was unclear whether they were officially cautioned and booked or not. The game was out of control at times, and Alf Ramsey called the Argentinians "Animals". There were scenes at the end of the match, as the referee needed a police escort, after having his shirt ripped by Roberto Ferreiro, and there were claims the referee had been manhandled and punched by a member of the Argentina backroom staff. And other punches were thrown at the England officials, including a spitting incident by Ermindo Onega against the FIFA vice-president Harry Cavan, in a show of disrespect by the South Americans, who felt cheated out of a chance to win the game. They played 60 minutes with 10 men. England got off scot-free. And it was claimed their goal by Hurst was offside. It was a shambles. But the result stood. And Alf Ramsey stopped his players from swapping their shirts with Argentina at the end, to signal his disgust. However, England were through to the World Cup semi final, to face Portugal.

Chapter Thirteen

The mods and rockers world tour continued, with the next stop being Florida, nicknamed "The Sunshine State", due to its warm climate and days of sunshine, which have attracted many northern migrants and vacationers since the 1920's.

The history of Florida can be traced back to when the first Native Americans began to inhabit the peninsula, as early as 14,000 years ago. They left behind various artefacts and archaeological evidence.

Florida's written history begins with the arrival of the Europeans. The Spanish explorer, Juan Ponce de Leon, in 1513, made the first textual records. The state received its name from this conquistador, who called the peninsula "La Pascua Florida", in recognition of the verdant, lush, green landscape, and because it was the Easter season, which the Spaniards called Pascua Florida (Festival of Flowers).

This area was the first mainland realm of the United States to be settled by the Europeans. Thus 1513 marked the beginning of the American frontier.

From that time of contact, Florida has had many waves of colonisation and immigration, including French and Spanish settlement during the 16th Century, as well as entry of the new Native American groups migrating from elsewhere in the south, and free blacks and fugitive slaves, who in the 19th Century became allied with the Native Americans, as Black Seminoles.

Florida was under colonial rule by Spain from the 16th Century to the 19th Century, and briefly by Great Britain during the 18th Century (1763-1783) before becoming a territory of the United States in 1821. Two decades later, Florida was admitted to the Union as the 27th U.S. state on March 3rd 1845.

The Jacksonville Coliseum, also known as the Jacksonville Veterans Memorial Coliseum was located at 1145E, Adams Street, Downtown Jacksonville, Florida, and was built in 1960, and known as the Sports Mecca of the South.

Today, it was hosting the mods and rockers pop concert, including Swagger the mods and Swagger the rockers. The capacity was 10, 276 and the place was full to the point of bursting.

The Coliseum was popular with music lovers and had hosted many concerts in the past, including Bob Dylan, Frank Sinatra, Jimi Hendrix, Elvis Presley and now The Who, The Rolling Stones, The Small Faces, Manfred Mann, Dave Dee, Dozy, Beaky, Mick and Tich, The Moody Blues, The Yardbirds, The Kinks, The

Troggs, The Spencer Davis Group and also The Beatles, who were joining the tour as special guests.

The first artist on the bill tonight were the go-go dancers, starting off the event with the number "Tell Him", which was released on the United Artists record label, on 21st February 1963, reaching number 46 and charting for one week, a song that was originally recorded by The Exciters.

"I know something about love
You've got to want it bad
If that guy's got into your blood
Go out and get him
If you want him to be
The very part of you
Make you want to breathe
Here's the thing to do
Tell him that you're never gonna leave him
Tell him that you're always gonna love him
Tell him, tell him, tell him, tell him right now
I know something about love
You gotta show it and
Make him see the moon up above
Go out and get him
If you want him to be
Always by your side
If you want him to
Only think of you
Tell him that you're never gonna leave him
Tell him that you're aways gonna love him
Tell him, tell him, tell him, tell him right now
Ever since the world began, it's been that way for man

And women were created
To make love their destiny
Then why should true love be so complicated, oh yeah?
I know something about love
You gotta take his hand
Show him what the world is made of
One kiss will prove it
If you want him to be
Always by your side
Take his hand tonight
Swallow your foolish pride
Tell him that you're never gonna leave him
Tell him that you're always gonna love him
Tell him, tell him, tell him, tell him right now
Oh, you have to tell him now (tell him that you're never gonna leave him)
Oh yeah, (tell him that you're always gonna love him)
Yeah, (tell him, tell him, tell him, tell him right now)
Darling, don't you let him go, now (tell him that you're never gonna leave him)
Oh yeah (tell him that you're always gonna love him)
Yeah, (tell him, tell him, tell him, tell him right now)
Take his hand in yours and tell him (tell him that you're never gonna leave him)
Oh yeah, (tell him that your always gonna love him)," sang the go-go dancers, with all six of them working in harmony, Jilly Jacobs, Jackie Jones, Rosie Wright, Becky Bright, Erica Shaw and Lily Lewis, doing their thing, with style, class, panache and personality.

The Florida crowd in the Jacksonville Coliseum loved the rendition by the beautiful English go-go dancers from Hull in East Yorkshire, and they showed their approval by whistling, cheering, applauding, screaming and shouting, and the ten thousand people in the audience sounded more like one hundred thousand, ten times the size, with the amount of noise and commotion they were generating.

The go-go dancers made their way to the front of the stage, to dance for the next artist, The Yardbirds, and they played "Shapes of Things", a track that was released on 3rd March 1966, on Columbia records, which reached number 3, and spent 9 weeks on the chart.

"Shapes of things before my eyes
Just teach me to despise
Will time make man more wise?
Here, within my lonely frame
My eyes just hurt my brain
But will it seem the same?
Come tomorrow, will I be older?
Come tomorrow, may be a soldier?
Come tomorrow, may I be bolder than today?
Now, the trees are almost green
But will they still be seen
When time and tide have been?
Falling into your passing hands
Please don't destroy these lands
Don't make them desert sands
Come tomorrow, will I be older?
Come tomorrow, maybe a soldier?
Come tomorrow, may I be bolder than today?

Soon I hope that I will find

Thoughts deep within my mind

That won't disgrace my kind," sang Keith Relf on lead vocals, with Jeff Beck on lead guitar and backing vocals, Jimmy Page on lead guitar and backing vocals, Jim McCory on drums and Paul Samwell-Smith on bass guitar. The Beck-Page double lead guitar fuzz box combo effect sounded brilliant.

The Jacksonville audience screamed with delight at the sensational performance by The Yardbirds, and the group thanked the crowd by bowing their heads and waving with appreciation. They left the stage and were replaced by The Beatles, with John Lennon, Paul McCartney, George Harrison and Ringo Starr taking the plaudits, which revved up the crowd into an ecstatic, frenzy of fanatical, fervour, as The Beatles started their first song, "I Feel Fine", which was released on 3rd December 1964, on the Parlophone record label, and the screaming, yelling, shouting and noise increased in volume, which was deafening. The women, young and old were letting this four piece music-combo from Liverpool really know they were loved.

"Baby's good to me, you know

She's happy as can be, you know

She said so

I'm in love with her and I feel fine

Baby says she's mine, you know

She tells me all the time, you know

She said so

I'm in love with her and I feel fine

I'm so glad that she's my little girl (ooh-ooh)

She's so glad she's telling all the world (ooh-ooh)

That her baby buys her things, you know

He buys her diamond rings, you know
She said so
She's in love with me and I feel fine
Guitar solo
Baby says she's mine, you know
She tells me all the time, you know
She said so
I'm in love with her and I feel fine
I'm so glad that she's my little girl (ooh-ooh)
She's so glad she's telling all the world (ooh-ooh)
That her baby buys her things, you know
He buys her diamond rings, you know
She said so
She's in love with me and I feel fine

She's in love with me and I feel fine," sang John Lennon on lead vocals and lead guitar, assisted by Paul McCartney on bass guitar and backing vocals, and Ringo Starr on drums, with George Harrison on lead and rhythm guitar, in what was a fantastic display of rock and blues, with an incredible feed back sound from the guitar, that pleased the crowd no end in the Jacksonville Coliseum. The reception to that song was startling and crazy, as the audience lifted the roof off the stadium. They loved it.

The Beatles continued with another track, "Paperback Writer". But before they could begin this song, the band needed to evacuate the stage, as a howling wind blew across the arena, taking speakers, drums, cymbals, microphones and amplifiers with it, as it whipped across the Coliseum.

The crowd screamed in horror, as the massive gusts blew in the glass from the windows, and everyone had to take cover. It was a tornado that had blown in from nowhere, and was raging and rampant, and it stopped the show.

Chapter Fourteen

The Beatles returned to the stage after a clean-up operation of the Jacksonville Coliseum, and all the loose items, such as drums, cymbals, microphone stands, speakers and amplifiers were nailed down by the stewards on duty.

There were no injuries among the crowd, so everyone was able to continue to enjoy the show, although the audience were anxious about any further turbulence from the weather.

When the Beatles started to play, the crowd soon forgot about the storm and they concentrated on the music. The next song, "Paperback Writer", was released on 16th June 1966, on the Parlophone record label, where it reached number 1, and spent 16 weeks on the chart.

 "Paperback writer (paperback writer)
  Dear Sir or Madam, will you read my book?
  It took me years to write, will you take a look?
  It's based on a novel by a man named Lear
  And I need a job
  So I wanna be a paperback writer (paperback writer)
  It's a dirty story of a dirty man
  And his clinging wife doesn't understand
  His son is working for The Daily Mail
  It's a steady job
  But he wants to be a paperback writer
  Paperback writer

Paperback writer (paperback writer)
It's a thousand pages give or take a few
I'll be writing more in a week or two
I could make it longer if you like the style
I can change it round
And I wanna be a paperback writer
Paperback writer
If you really like it you can have the rights
It could make a million for you overnight
If you must return it you can send it here
But I need a break
And I wanna be a paperback writer
Paperback writer
Paperback writer (paperback writer)
Paperback writer (paperback writer)
Paperback writer (paperback writer)
Paperback writer (paperback writer)
Paperback writer (paperback writer)," sang Paul McCartney on lead vocals and bass guitar, John Lennon on rhythm guitar and backing vocals, George Harrison on lead guitar and rhythm guitar and Ringo Starr on drums.
The Beatles continued with another song, as the crowd shrieked in appreciation, howling, screaming, yelling and applauding, and the noise was so loud and vociferous that the band were almost drowned out. The next song was "Day Tripper", and it was welcomed by the fervent crowd with open arms. This track was released on 9th December 1965, on the Parlophone record label, reaching number 1 and charting for 12 weeks.
"Got a good reason
For taking the easy way out

Got a good reason

For taking the easy way out, now

She was a day tripper

One way ticket, yeah

It took me so long to find out

And I found out

She's a big teaser

She took me half the way there

She's a big teaser

She took me half the way there, now

She was a day tripper

One way ticket yeah

It took me so long to find out

And I found out

Ah, ah, ah, ah, ah, ah, ah (guitar solo)

Tried to please her

She only played one night stand

Tried to please her

She only played one night stand, now

She was a day tripper

Sunday driver yeah

It took me so long to find out

And I found out

Day tripper, day tripper yeah

Day tripper, day tripper yeah," sang John Lennon on lead vocals and rhythm guitar, Paul McCartney on backing vocals and bass guitar, Ringo Starr on drums and George Harrison on lead guitar.

The crowd were louder than ever in their applause and appreciation, and they brought the house down. The tornado may have subsided and disappeared, but the crowd made up for the storm, with their keen, energetic reception, and The Beatles bowed and waved and smiled in response, before moving onto their next song, "Ticket to Ride", which was released on 15th April 1965, on the Parlophone record label, that reached number 1 and charted for 14 weeks.

"I think I'm gonna be sad
I think it's today, yeah
The girl that's driving me mad
Is going away
She's got a ticket to ride
She's got a ticket to ride
She's got a ticket to ride
But she don't care
She said that living with me
Is bringing her down, yeah
For she would never be free
When I was around
She's got a ticket to ride
She's got a ticket to ride
She's got a ticket to ride
But she don't care
I don't know why she's ridin' so high
She ought to think twice
She ought to do right by me
Before she gets to saying goodbye
She ought to think twice
She ought to do right by me
I think I'm gonna be sad
I think it's today, yeah

The girl that's driving me mad
Is going away, yeah
Ah, she's got a ticket to ride
She's got a ticket to ride
She's got a ticket to ride
But she don't care
I don't know why she's ridin' so high
She ought to think twice
She ought to do right by me
Before she gets to saying goodbye
She ought to think twice
She ought to do right by me
She said that living with me
Is bringing her down, yeah
For she would never be free
When I was around
Ah, she's got a ticket to ride
She's got a ticket to ride
She's got a ticket to ride
But she don't care
My baby don't care
My baby don't care
My baby don't care
My baby don't care," sang John Lennon on lead vocals and rhythm guitar, Paul McCartney on backing vocals and bass guitar, Ringo Starr on drums, and George Harrison on lead guitar and backing vocals.
The crowd whooped. The girls were fainting with hysteria, as the occasion was too much for them. The moment was magic to the females. The beat was strong. The harmonies were perfect.

The sound of the guitars were sweet. The drumming was driving. It was musical perfection, and although live, it was just as good as the vinyl record.

The next track performed by The Beatles was "A Hard Day's Night", which was released on 16th July 1964, reaching number 1, and was in the charts for 15 weeks, and on the Parlophone record label.

"It's been a hard day's night and I've been working like a dog
It's been a hard day's night, I should be sleeping like a log
But when I get home to you, I'll find the things that you do
Will make me feel alright
You know I work all day, to get you money to buy you things
And it's worth it just to hear you say, you're going to give me everything
So why on earth should I moan, 'cause when I get you alone
You know I feel okay
When I'm home, everything seems to be right
When I'm home, feeling you holding me tight, tight, yeah
It's been a hard day's night and I've been working like a dog
It's been a hard day's night, I should be sleeping like a log
But when I get home to you, I find the things that you do
Will make me feel alright, oww
Guitar solo
So why on earth should I moan, 'cause when I get you alone
You know I feel okay
When I'm home everything seems to be right
When I'm home feeling you holding me tight, tight, yeah
Oh, it's been a hard day's night and I've been working like a dog
It's been a hard day's night, I should be sleeping like a log

But when I get home to you, I'll find the things that you do
Will make me feel alright
You know I feel alright
You know I feel alright," sang John Lennon on lead vocals and on rhythm guitar, Paul McCartney on bass guitar and backing vocals, Ringo Starr on drums, and George Harrison on lead guitar and additional backing vocals.

It was fabulous, immense, awesome, with a driving beat, great harmony, perfect pitch, fantastic melody and the best song of the night from The Beatles, which the crowd of over ten thousand greatly appreciated.

The band left the stage to a standing ovation, and were replaced by The Troggs, who played their hit "With A Girl Like You", that was released on 14th July 1966, which reached number 1, and spent 12 weeks on the chart, and was on the Fontana record label.

"I want to spend my life with a girl like you
Ba, ba, ba, ba, ba, ba, ba, ba, ba
And do all the things that you want me to
Ba, ba, ba, ba, ba, ba, ba, ba, ba
Till that time has come that we might live as one
Can I dance with you?
Ba, ba, ba, ba, ba, ba, ba, ba, ba
Ba, ba, ba, ba, ba, ba, ba, ba, ba
I tell by the way you dress, that you're so refined
Ba, ba, ba, ba, ba, ba, ba, ba, ba
And by the way you talk that you're just my kind
Ba, ba, ba, ba, ba, ba, ba, ba, ba
Girl, why should it be, that you don't notice me?
Can I dance with you?

Ba, ba, ba, ba, ba, ba, ba, ba, ba

Ba, ba, ba, ba, ba, ba, ba, ba, ba

Baby, baby, is there no chance

I can take you for the last dance?

All night long, yeah, I've been waiting

Now they'll be no hesitating

So, before this dance has reached the end

Ba, ba, ba, ba, ba, ba, ba, ba, ba

To you across the floor, my love I'll send

Ba, ba, ba, ba, ba, ba, ba, ba, ba

I just hope and pray that I'll find a way to say

Can I dance with you?

Ba, ba, ba, ba, ba, ba, ba, ba, ba

Ba, ba, ba, ba, ba, ba, ba, ba, ba," sang Reg Presley on lead vocals, Ronnie Bond on drums, Pete Staples on bass guitar and backing vocals, and Chris Britton on lead guitar and vocal backing.

Chapter Fifteen

The concert at the Jacksonville Coliseum ended on a high. The crowd erupted with joy, as The Troggs completed the show, and The Beatles, The Yardbirds and the go-go dancers appeared alongside Swagger the mods and Swagger the rockers, The Who, The Rolling Stones, The Kinks and The Small Faces, for a quick finale, before the tornado storm returned with a vengeance and the musicians headed off the stage to much applause and cheering from the brave audience, before a large gust of wind engulfed the arena to create more panic and mayhem.

The USA tour continued and the entourage were jetting off to New York as soon as the storm settled down, and heading for the Shea Stadium, which was also known as the William A Shea Municipal Stadium, that was a multi-purpose stadium in Flushing Meadows, Corona Park, Queens, New York City.

It had been built as a multi-purpose stadium and was the home park of Major League Baseball's New York Mets from 1964, as well as the New York Jets football team. The stadium was opened on 17th April 1964 at the cost of $28.5 million dollars, which was $238 million dollars in today's money.

The venue was named in honour of William Shea, the man who was instrumental for bringing National League Baseball back to New York, after the Dodgers and Giants left for California in May 1957. It was originally going to be called The Flushing Meadows Municipal Stadium, the name of the public park within which it was built. But an ultimately successful movement was launched to name it in honour of William A Shea.

The history of New York City began around 10,000 BC. In 1664, England renamed the colony New York after the Duke of York and Albany, the brother of King Charles II. And New York City gained prominence in the 18th Century as a major trading port in the Thirteen Colonies.

It all began with the first European explorer, the Italian, Giovanni de Verrazzano, in 1524. European settlement began with the Dutch in 1608, and in 1656 the population was 1000, in 1810 the population was 96,000, in 1890 the population was 1.5 million and in 1960 the population was 7 million.

"The Sons of Liberty" campaign against British authority in New York City and the Stamp Act Congress of representatives from throughout the Thirteen Colonies met in the city in 1776, to organise resistance to Crown Policies.

The Thirteen Colonies were a group of British Colonies on the Atlantic coast of North America. Founded in the 17th and 18th Centuries, they began fighting the American Revolutionary war in April 1775 and formed the United States of America by declaring independence on 4th July 1776.

New York, New Jersey, Pennsylvania and Delaware were in the middle part of the colonies. These middle colonies were established on an earlier Dutch colony, New Netherlands, which became part of New York.

In 1898, the modern city of New York was formed, with the consolidation of Brooklyn, Manhattan and The Bronx. With Queens County established, along with Nassau in 1899, which bordered the borough of Queens. New York played a pivotal role during the American Revolution, and the subsequent war.

The Stamp Act Congress in 1765 brought together representatives from across the Thirteen Colonies, to form a unified response to British policies. The Battle of Saratoga was the turning point in the war, in favour of the Americans, after convincing France to ally with them. New York's constitution was adopted in 1777 and strongly influenced the United States constitution.

The Hollies joined the tour of the USA and played first in the concert at the Shea Stadium in New York City, and they started off the gig with "I'm Alive", which was released on 27th May 1965, and reached number 1, charting for 14 weeks, and was on the Parlophone record label.

The go-go dancers were at the front of the stage and were dressed in white bikinis, as the weather was warm, and they were strutting their stuff with charm, charisma, aplomb and panache, just like they always did. The crowd was 55,000 strong, although they seemed to be more than that. The stadium was packed to the rafters.

"Did you ever see a man with no heart?
Baby, that was me
Just a lonely, lonely man with no heart
'til you set me free
Now I can breathe
I can see
I can touch
I can feel
I can taste all the sugar sweetness in your kiss
You give me all the things I've ever missed
I've never felt like this
I'm alive, I'm alive, I'm alive
I used to think that I was living
Baby, I was wrong
No, I never knew a thing about living
'til you came along
Now I can breathe
I can see
I can touch
I can feel
I can taste all the sugar sweetness in your kiss
You gave me all the things I've ever missed
I've never felt like this
I'm alive, I'm alive, I'm alive
Guitar solo
Now I can breathe

I can see

I can touch

I can feel

I can taste all the sugar sweetness in your kiss

You gave me all the love I've ever missed

I've never felt like this

I'm alive, I'm alive, I'm alive

I'm alive, I'm alive," sang Allan Clark on lead vocals, Graham Nash on rhythm guitar, Eric Haydock on bass guitar, Tony Hicks on lead guitar and backing vocals and Bobby Elliott on drums.

The crowd gave the group a resounding round of applause, huge cheers, screaming, and calls of "More, more, more". The Hollies promptly obliged by going into another number. "Just One Look", that reached number 2, charted for 13 weeks, and was released on the Parlophone record label, on 27th February 1964.

"Just one look

That's all it took, yeah

Just one look

That's all it took, yeah

Just one look

And I felt so I, I, I'm in love, with you

Oh, oh

I found out

How good it feels, feels, feels

To have, your love

Oh, oh

Say you will

Will be mine, mine, mine

Forever, and always

Oh, oh

Just one look
And I knew, knew, knew
That you, were my only one
Oh, oh, whoa
I thought I was dreaming
But I was wrong, yeah, yeah, yeah
Oh, but I'm gonna keep on scheming
'til I can make you
Make you my own
So you see
I really care, care, care
Without you, I'm nothing
Oh, oh
Just one look
And I know
Oh, oh
I'll get you, someday
Oh, oh, whoa
I thought I was dreaming
But I was wrong, yeah, yeah, yeah
Oh, but I'm gonna keep on scheming
'til I can make you
Make you my own
Just one look
That's all it took, yeah
Just one look
That's all it took, yeah
Just one look
That's all it took, yeah
Just one look

That's all it took, yeah

Just one look," sang Allan Clark on lead vocals, Graham Nash on rhythm guitar, Eric Haydock on bass guitar, Tony Hicks on lead guitar and backing vocals, and Bobby Elliott on drums.

The audience screamed with passionate delight, showing their appreciation to The Hollies, with gratefulness. The music continued and the next song performed by The Hollies was "Look Through Any Window", which was released on 2nd September 1965, on Parlophone records, which reached number 4, charting for 11 weeks.

"Look through any window, yeah
What do you see?
Smilin' faces all around
Rushin' through the busy town
(Where do they go?)
Movin' on their way
Walkin' down the highways and the byways
(Where do they go?)
Movin' on their way
People with their shy ways and their sly ways
Oh, you can see the little children
All around
Oh, you can see the little ladies
In their gowns, when you
Look through any window, yeah
Any time of day
See the drivers on the road
Pullin' down their heavy loads
(Where do they go?)
Movin' on their way

Drivin' down the highways and the byways

(Where do they go)

Movin' on their way

Drivers with their shy ways and their sly ways

Oh, you can see the little children

All around

Oh, you can see the little ladies

In their gowns, when you

Look through any window, yeah

What do you see?

Smilin' faces all around

Rushin' through the busy town

Movin' on their way

Movin' on their way

Movin' on their way," sang Allan Clark on lead vocals, Graham Nash on rhythm guitar, Eric Haydock on bass guitar, Tony Hicks on lead guitar and backing vocals, and Bobby Elliott on drums.

The crowd gave a hot reception to this track, as they loved it. It got everyone dancing, grooving and rocking, and the go-go dancers led the way with some groovy shapes and shuffles of their own, encouraging everyone.

And the music just kept on coming, fast and furious with The Hollies, and they played another one of their fantastic hit songs, "Bus Stop", which was released on 23rd June 1966, reaching number 5, charting for 9 weeks, and was recorded on the Parlophone record label.

"Bus stop, wet day, she's there, I say

"Please share my umbrella"

Bus stop, bus goes, she stays, love grows

Under my umbrella

All that summer, we enjoyed it
Wind and rain and shine
That umbrella, we employed it
By August, she was mine
Every morning, I would see her waiting at the stop
Sometimes she'd shopped and she would show me what she'd bought
All the people stared as if we were both quite insane
Someday my name and her's are going to be the same
That's the way the whole thing started
Silly but it's true
Thinkin' of a sweet romance
Beginning in a queue
Came the sun, the ice was melting
No more sheltering now
Nice to think that that umbrella
Led me to a vow
Every mornin', I would see her waiting at the stop
Sometimes she'd shopped and she would show me what she'd bought
All the people stared as if we were both quite insane
Someday my name and her's are going to be the same
Bus stop, wet day, she's there, I say
"Please share my umbrella"
Bus stop, bus goes, she stays, love grows under my umbrella
All that summer we enjoyed it
Wind and rain and shine
That umbrella, we employed it

By August, she was mine," sang Allan Clark on lead vocals, Graham Nash on rhythm guitar, Eric Haydock on bass guitar, Tony Hicks on lead guitar and Bobby Elliott on drums.

The song was fantastic, and was well received by the crowd, who cheered, applauded, screamed and yelled their approval, as The Hollies finished their set.

Chapter Sixteen

The quarter final results in the 1966 World Cup were as follows;
England 1 Argentina 0
West Germany 4 Uruguay 0
USSR 2 Hungary 1
Portugal 5 North Korea 3
The game everyone had been waiting for in the United Kingdom, England v Portugal, had arrived, in the semi final of the World Cup, at Wembley, on Tuesday 26th July 1966, with a 7.30 pm kick off, British Summer Time.

The attendance inside the stadium was 94, 493, with television beaming it across the nation on BBC One and ITV, including ATV, Border, Grampian, Granada, Rediffusion, Tyne Tees, Scottish, Ulster, Westward, Anglia, Southern, Cymru and TWW channels.

England lined up as follows;

1, Gordon Banks, Leicester City, goalkeeper

2, George Cohen, Fulham, right full back

3, Ray Wilson, Everton, left full back

4, Nobby Stiles, Manchester United, midfield

5, Jack Charlton, Leeds United, central defender

6, Bobby Moore, West Ham United, central defender, captain

7, Alan Ball, Blackpool, midfield

21, Roger Hunt, Liverpool, forward

9, Bobby Charlton, Manchester United, attacking midfield

10, Geoff Hurst, West Ham United, forward

16, Martin Peters, West Ham United, midfield

Portugal took to the field with this team;

3, Jose Pereira, Belenenses CF, goalkeeper

9, Hilario, Sporting CP, left full back

20, Alexandre Baptista, Sporting CP, central defender

21, Jose Carlos, Sporting CP, central defender

22, Alberto Festa, Porto, right full back

10, Mario Coluna, Benfica, midfield, captain

16, Jaime Graca, Benfica, midfield

11, Antonio Simoes, Benfica, left winger

12, Jose Augusto, Benfica, right winger

13, Eusebio, Benfica, forward

18, Jose Torres, Benfica, forward

This match was the match of all matches. A classic in its own right. It was scintillating to watch. Action packed. Skilled. Superb. Sublime. Sensational.

The style of football was brilliant, which was entertaining, enthralling, exciting, and edge of the seat quality. Bobby Charlton was the star of the show, with two brilliant goals, which won the match for England, and put them through into the World Cup Final.

Bobby Charlton was on another planet, playing with power, precision and grace, and moving around the pitch like a panther. One goal was drilled high into the net from 25 yards and the other rifled low into the goal, following a blocked shot from a

Roger Hunt effort, which Charlton pounced on from the rebound.

England conceded a goal seven minutes from full time, following a handball by Jack Charlton from a Jose Torres header, which Eusebio dispatched into the net with ease. This was the first goal conceded by England in the tournament. But Portugal didn't look like scoring from open play, with Gordon Banks covering his goal exceptionally well, and Nobby Stiles marshalling Eusebio superbly, in a disciplined, defensive effort. It was a disappointing night for Eusebio, who was fresh from his stunning 4 goals performance in the quarter final against North Korea, as Portugal came back from 3-0 down in that game, to win 5-3.

But the night belonged to England, and in particular to Bobby Charlton, with his crucial two goals, that booked England a place in the 1966 World Cup Final.

Eusebio left the pitch in tears, as the two teams got a standing ovation, and cries of "When The Whites Go Marching In" was ringing around the Wembley Stadium, celebrating England's classic semi final victory.

England wore the 1965/66 Umbro white crew necked jerseys, blue shorts and white socks, whilst Portugal's kit was maroon jerseys, with green collar and cuffs, white shorts, with red side trim and green socks. Their manager was Manuel da Luz Afonso. The referee was Pierre Schwinte from France. And Alf Ramsey was the England manager. Bobby Charlton's goals were in the 31st and 79th minutes, with Eusebio's penalty in the 83rd minute. The game would live long in the memory of every England supporter for many years to come.

The entourage jetted off from New York to their next destination, Canada, for the latest leg of the Mods and Rockers

World Wide Tour. The Maple Leaf Gardens, located at the northwest corner of Carlton Street and Church Street in Toronto, Ontario was the venue. This building was initially constructed in 1931 as an arena to host ice hockey games, though it has since been reconstructed for other uses, such as this 1966 Mods and Rockers World Tour show, which held 15,000 people for the legendary music gig.

It was one of the few venues outside the United States where Elvis Presley performed in concert, in April 1957. But today, it was holding The Dave Clark Five pop group from England and The Who, The Rolling Stones, The Small Faces, The Kinks, Swagger the mods, Swagger the rockers, the go-go dancers and The Beatles, for a music extravaganza.

Dave Clark Five were the first on the stage, with their hit song "Glad All Over", recorded on the Columbia record label on 21st November 1963, which charted for 19 weeks and reached number 1.

"You say that you love me (say you love me)
All of the time (all of the time)
You say that you need me (say you need me)
You'll always be mine (always be mine)
I'm feelin' (glad all over)
Yes, I'm-a (glad all over)
Baby, I'm (glad all over)
So glad you're mine
I'll make you happy (make you happy)
You'll never be blue (never be blue)
You'll have no sorrow (have no sorrow)
'cause I'll always be true (always be true)
And I'm feelin' (glad all over)

Yes, I'm-a (glad all over)
Baby, I'm (glad all over)
So glad (you're mine)
Other girls may try to take me away (take me away)
But you know, it's by your side I will stay (I'll stay)
Our love will last now (our love will last)
'til the end of time (end of time)
Because this love now (because this love)
Is only yours and mine (yours and mine)
And I'm feelin' (glad all over)
Yes, I'm-a (glad all over)
Baby, I'm (glad all over)
So glad (you're mine)
Other girls may try to take me away (take me away)
But you know, it's by your side I will stay (I'll stay)
Our love will last now (our love will last)
'til the end of time (end of time)
Because this love now (because this love)
Is only yours and mine (yours and mine)
And I'm feelin' (glad all over)
Yes, I'm-a (glad all over)
Baby, I'm (glad all over)
So glad you're mine
I'm so glad you're mine now
I'm so glad you're mine
I'm so glad you're mine now
Whoa-whoa-whoa-whoa-whoa," sang Mike Smith on lead vocals and keyboards, Dave Clark on drums and backing vocals, Lenny Davidson on guitar and backing vocals, Denis Payton on

saxophone and backing vocals and Rick Huxley on guitar and backing vocals.

The crowd in Toronto loved it. The Maple Leaf Gardens rocked and was bouncing. The Dave Clark Five proved to be very popular in Canada. The go-go dancers paraded and cavorted at the front of the stage, wearing gold and black striped bikinis, as the weather was lovely and warm, and the dancers showed off their beautiful golden suntans, and were also lovely and warm.

The next song by The Dave Clark Five was "Bits and Pieces", which was recorded on Columbia records, charted for 11 weeks, reached number 2, and was released on 20th February 1964. The crowd howled with delight, showing their approval to this track, as it was a great dance number, to jiggle and wiggle to.

"(I'm in pieces, bits and pieces) since you left me and you said goodbye

(I'm in pieces, bits and pieces) all I do is sit and cry

(I'm in pieces, bits and pieces) you went away and left me misery

(I'm in pieces, bits and pieces) and that's the way it'll always be

(I'm in pieces, bits and pieces) you said you loved me and you'd always be mine

(I'm in pieces, bits and pieces) we'd be together 'til the end of time

(I'm in pieces, bits and pieces) now you say it was just a game

(I'm in pieces, bits and pieces) but all you're doin' is leaving me pain

Time goes by, and goes so slow (oh yeah)

It just doesn't seem true

Only just a few days ago

You said you'd love me, never make me blue

(I'm in pieces, bits and pieces) now you've gone and I'm all alone

(I'm in pieces, bits and pieces) and you're still way up there on your throne

(I'm in pieces, bits and pieces) oh, nothing seems to ever go right

(I'm in pieces, bits and pieces) 'cause night is day and day is night," sang Mike Smith on lead vocals and keyboards, Dave Clark on drums and backing vocals, Lenny Davidson on guitar and backing vocals, Denis Paton on saxophone and backing vocals and Rick Huxley on guitar and backing vocals.

The crowd cheered, screamed and yelled their approval. The beat bounced. The stadium bounced. The audience bounced. The song was fantastic, incredible and immense. The go-go dancers continued to strut their sexy stuff and grinded with style and panache, oozing passion and sensuality.

The next song was "Catch Us If You Can", a track that was released on 15th July, 1965, on the Columbia record label, which reached number 5, and charted for 11 weeks.

"Here they come again, hmmm

Catch us if you can, hmmm

Time to get a move on, hmmm

We will yell with all of our might

Catch us if you can, catch us if you can, catch us if you can, catch us if you can

Now we gotta run, hmmm

No more time for fun, hmmm

When we're getting angry, hmmm

We will yell with all of our might

Catch us if you can, catch us if you can, catch us if you can, catch us if you can

Woah, harmonica solo

Here they come again, hmmm

Catch us if you can, hmmm

Time to get a move on, hmmm

We will yell with all of our might

Catch us if you can, catch us if you can, catch us if you can, catch us if you can," sang Mike Smith on lead vocals and keyboards, Dave Clark on drums and backing vocals, Lenny Davidson on guitar and backing vocals, Denis Paton on saxophone and harmonica, and Rick Huxley on guitar and backing vocals.

The audience raised the roof. The sound was loud and fantastic. The beat was glorious. The harmony was great, and the crowd showed their approval with non-stop applauding, screaming, stamping of their feet and created noise aplenty.

Chapter Seventeen

The day had arrived for the final of the World Cup 1966. In all its splendour and pomp. The semi finals of the tournament had been completed and the results were as follows;

England 2 Portugal 1

West Germany 2 USSR 1

Meaning England would play West Germany at Wembley on Saturday 30th July 1966, to contest the Jules Rimet Trophy, otherwise known as the World Cup. The most famous and prestigious tournament in world football. Nothing compared to winning the Jules Rimet Trophy. So much so, that the trophy went missing.

On Sunday 20th March, four months before the World Cup Final, the Jules Rimet Trophy was on display at the Methodist Central Hall, Westminster. The Football Association had usually kept the trophy in their headquarters at Lancaster Gate, under lock and key, and out of the public eye. But Stanley Gibbons Stamp Company received permission to place the trophy in their Stampex Exhibition, on condition it would be under guard at all times. The trophy was insured for £30,000, despite its official value being only £3,000.

The World Cup was the major attraction from the first day, on Saturday 19th March 1966, as two uniformed officers guarded the trophy round the clock, reinforced by two plainclothes officers during the day. Additional guards stood beside the cabinet when the exhibition was open, but nobody was watching the trophy all of the time.

On Sunday's, the Central Hall was used for Methodist Services, and on Sunday 20th March, when the guards began a noon circuit, around 12.10pm, they noticed that someone had forced the display cabinet open, and the rear doors of the building, and had stolen the Jules Rimet Trophy. The wooden bar that had held the door closed was lying on the floor, along with the screws and bolts from the brackets that had held the bar securely. The thieves had removed the padlock from the back of the display case, taken the trophy and left the same way they came. In broad daylight. None of the guards had seen or heard anything suspicious, though one of them reported that he had seen a strange man by the public telephone, when he had visited the toilet on the first floor.

Scotland Yard took control of the case and gave it to Flying Squad officers, who in turn interviewed the guards and two maintenance workers. One of the churchgoers had also noticed a man and gave a different description. The story went public across the world the next day, and the police looked for two potential suspects, although the description the newspapers provided, did not correspond to either of the men the witnesses had seen.

On Monday 21st March, Joe Mears, the chairman of the Football Association received an anonymous telephone call. The unknown man said that Mears would receive a parcel at Chelsea Football Club, the next day. The parcel was delivered to Mear's home. It contained the removable lining from the top of the trophy and a ransom note that demanded £15,000 in £1 and £5 notes, and mentioned leaving a coded advertisement in the personal ads in The Evening News, and not to involve the police. It got complicated. The man then changed his request for £5 and £10 notes. If the FA followed further instructions, they could get the trophy back by Friday. But if they involved the police, the thieves threatened to melt the trophy down. Mears went to the police and they filled a suitcase with plain paper, and real money at the top and bottom, with two police officers acting as Mears assistants.

It was a futile pursuit, as this mystery man going under the name of "Jackson" got scared and nervous, when arranging the exhange of cash for the trophy at Battersea Park, and the police arrested him, after he jumped from a moving vehicle in a panic, after agreeing to lead the police officers to the trophy. The man, whose real name was Edward Betchley was convicted of theft and breaking and entering, and sentenced to two years in prison, but died of emphysema in 1969. He denied stealing the cup, and always claimed to be the middle man for "The Pole". And he said he had been offered £500. The church witness, Mrs Coombes identified him, although the security guard did not recognise him.

After all the hullabaloo of coded ads in the Evening News, suitcases full of plain paper and lies and deceit, the Jules Rimet Trophy was still missing.

On 27th March, a week after it had been stolen, David Corbett and his dog, a Border collie, called Pickles, were walking in the Beulah Hill district of southeast London, when Pickles began to sniff at a parcel that was lying under the hedge of Corbett's house. It was wrapped in old newspaper, tied with string and contained the famous World Cup, with the winners names engraved at the bottom.

Mr Corbett informed the police and was briefly suspected of theft, but had an alibi. Pickles became a celebrity overnight. And Corbett received rewards totalling £6,000 from private sources, although he didn't receive anything from the Football Association. It was more than England were being paid in bonuses, if they won the World Cup. The FA made a replica of the trophy for further public displays, after this incident, and the police announced the recovery of the trophy the next day, but retained the cup as evidence until 18th April, and returned it to the FA in time for the tournament.

The 1966 FIFA World Cup Final between England and West Germany was ready to kick off. The referee was Gottfried Dienst from Switzerland. The spectators inside Wembley were singing themselves hoarse. There was an amazing atmosphere in the air, as 96,924 had packed inside the stadium. The United

Kingdom's television audience peaked at 32.3 million, making it the UK's most watched television event ever. And on top of that, 400 million worldwide were tuning in to this event. England were managed by Alf Ramsey and captained by Bobby Moore, and he won the toss and elected to kick off. England lined up like this;

1, Gordon Banks, Leicester City, aged 28, goalkeeper

2, George Cohen, Fulham, aged 26, right full back

3, Ray Wilson, Everton, aged 31, left full back

4, Nobby Stiles, Manchester United, aged 24, midfield

5, Jack Charlton, Leeds United, aged 31, central defender

6, Bobby Moore, captain, West Ham United, aged 25, central defender

7, Alan Ball, Blackpool, aged 21, midfield

21, Roger Hunt, Liverpool, aged 28, centre forward

9, Bobby Charlton, Manchester United, aged 28, attacking midfield

10, Geoff Hurst, aged 24, West Ham United, centre forward

16, Martin Peters, aged 22, West Ham United, midfield

The linesmen were Tofiq Bahramov from Azerbaijan and Karol Galba from Czechoslovakia. England wore red crew necked jerseys, white shorts and red socks. West Germany wore white shirts, with black trim, black shorts and white socks.

Germany lined up as follows;

1, Hans Tilkowski, Borussia Dortmund, aged 31, goalkeeper

2, Horst-Dieter Hottges. Werder Bremen, aged 23, right full back

3, Karl-Heinz Schnellinger, AC Milan, aged 27, left full back

4, Franz Beckenbauer, Bayern Munich, aged 20, central defender and sweeper

5, Willi Schulz, Hamburger SV, aged 27, central defender

6, Wolfgang Weber, FC Koln, aged 22, central defender

12, Wolfgang Overath, FC Koln, aged 22, midfield

8, Helmut Haller, Bologna FC, aged 27, right wing

9, Uwe Seeler, captain, Hamburger SV, aged 29, centre forward

10, Sigfried Held, Borussia Dortmund, aged 23, centre forward

11, Lothar Emmerich, Borussia Dortmund, aged 24, left wing

The West Germany manager was Helmut Schon.

The national anthems played before the game kicked off and the Queen, dressed in yellow was present, sitting next to the FIFA president Stanley Rous.

The noise was loud, creating an incredible atmosphere, as the England supporters were in full voice. They watched as the captains exchanged trinkets, with Uwe Seeler handing Bobby Moore a shiny, tapered pennant, with his Football Association's logo on it, and the England captain Bobby Moore presented Uwe Seeler with a plain, brown square-shaped folded carton, that was similar to a hardbound book. There was rain before the game, which left the pitch wet, soggy and soft, like a quagmire. And cries of "England! England! England!" were still being heard around the packed stadium.

In the 12th minute, West Germany scored the opening goal, after a cross by Sigfried Held was only half cleared by Ray Wilson, who made a basic error and gifted the ball to Helmut Haller, with a misdirected header, and Haller got his shot on target to put West Germany 1-0 up. Bobby Moore had been alert to the danger and closed Haller down, in an attempt to block the shot, but failed, and Jack Charlton and Gordon Banks also failed to deal with the shot, but Haller was deadly in the penalty area, and he didn't make any mistake, striking with precision, in a clinical manner.

In the 18th minute, Wolfgang Overath conceded a free kick, which Bobby Moore took immediately, floating a cross into the West Germany penalty area, where Geoff Hurst rose high, unchallenged, and glanced a downward header into the net, levelling the scores at 1-1. The West Germany goalkeeper failed to come for the cross, having been clattered by Geoff Hurst a few minutes earlier, with a body check, elbow and shoulder to the face, which had knocked him out cold, temporarily, and it had an effect on his confidence. The challenge by Hurst was hard and arguably dirty. But the England forward received a blow to the eye in the process, so it was fifty-fifty, although Tilkowski came off worse. Nothing much happened for the duration of the first half, with plenty of effort and hard work, but no end results. The half time whistle was blown and the score was still tied at 1-1.

In the 77th minute, England won a corner, with Alan Ball delivering a cross to Geoff Hurst, whose deflected shot from the edge of the area found Martin Peters. He produced a drilled shot, that beat the West Germany goalkeeper, Tilkowski, from 8 yards, to give England a 2-1 lead. West Germany pressed for an equaliser in the closing minutes, and Jack Charlton conceded a free kick in the 89th minute, after climbing on Uwe Seeler, as they both went up for a header.

The kick was taken by Lothar Emmerich, who struck it into George Cohen in the wall, the rebound fell to Sigfried Held, who shot across the face of the goal and into the body of Karl-Heinz Schnellinger. The ball deflected across the England six-yard box, wrong-footing the England defence, allowing Wolfgang

Weber to level the score at 2-2, and force the game into extra-time. Gordon Banks protested that the ball had struck Schnellinger on the arm, but replays showed it hit Schnellinger on the back.

Bobby Charlton hit the post with a shot in extra-time and hit another shot just wide. Alan Ball sent over a cross and Geoff Hurst swivelled and shot from close range. The ball hit the underside of the crossbar, bounced down and was cleared. The referee was unsure if had crossed the line, and consulted the linesman, Tofiq Bahramov from Azerbaijan, who indicated that it had crossed the line, and a goal was awarded. 3-2 to England, after 101 minutes.

The goal was controversial. There were plenty of theories. Some Germans reckoned the linesman was biased, following USSR's elimination by West Germany in the semi final. Even though he was from Azerbaijan. Some fans stated the ball was on the line, and needed to be fully over the line. But it didn't matter. As one minute before the final whistle, Bobby Moore picked out Geoff Hurst with a long pass, which Hurst dribbled forward, with spectators coming onto the pitch to celebrate. But Hurst continued to run, with the ball at his feet, and hammer a shot as hard and as high as he possibly could, to waste time. But he mis-hit the shot, as it went straight into the top corner of Hans Tilkowski's net, sealing a historic hat-trick and winning the World Cup for England. The goal gave rise to one of England's most iconic football phrases in history, when the BBC commentator Kenneth Wolstenholme described the situation as follows, "And here comes Hurst, he's got.......some people are on the pitch, they think it's all over. It is now! It's four!"

The End

Printed in Great Britain
by Amazon

39455491R00076